CW00725812

Cash

The love child of an Austrian prince and a 60's top model. Candy Barr was educated at a convent in Surrey and a finishing school in Switzerland. At the age of fourteen she landed her first film role, in Luigi Fettucine's controversial musical, 'Night of the Living Zombies'. Although on the threshold of movie stardom, she sacrificed her film career to devote herself fully to the life of the jet-set novelist. She now lives in Bel Air, Gstaad and Monaco with three borzois and a bird of paradise.

Candy Barr claims her heroine and literary mentor to be the writer Caroline Bridgwood, whose novels *This Wicked Generation*, *The Dew of Heaven* and *Magnolia Gardens* are also published by Pan Books.

Candy Barr

Cash

Pan Original
Pan Books London Sydney and Auckland

First published 1988 by Pan Books Ltd,
Cavaye Place, London SW10 9PG

9 8 7 6 5 4 3 2 1

© Caroline Bridgwood

ISBN 0 330 3054 2

Printed and bound in Great Britain by Richard Clay Ltd, Bungay, Suffolk

To my brother
John (Shuff)

One

'So, m'dear, this is our strategy . . .'

In the Newgate Street offices of Boeler Sute, one of the City of London's leading merchant banks, Oliver Riddle was in a meeting with his personnel manager, Tanya Dowling.

Oliver Riddle was forty-four and head of the bank's expanding corporate finance division, which meant that he was very important indeed. Tanya Dowling was only twenty-seven and a woman, and therefore not very important at all, but she was in charge of the bank's graduate recruitment drive and now, in March, it was time for her to co-ordinate the storming of Britain's most prestigious educational establishments. She and Riddle were leaving that evening for Cambridge, where they would spend two nights at a five star hotel running up gargantuan expenses, and two days interviewing the young hopefuls who aspired to the fat pickings of the City.

Tanya moved away from the smoked glass window where she had been standing, looking down twelve floors to the street below. As she brushed past Riddle's chair, he gave her left buttock a subtle, paternalistic pat. So subtle, she barely felt it, yet her face coloured up prettily.

'Where was I?' asked Riddle, smiling at her as she sat down opposite him. 'Ah yes. So we're not going to go in there and give the little blighters a hard sell. Should be no need. The sort of man . . . Sorry—' He gave her another patronising smile, 'Correction: the sort of *person* we're after will know enough about merchant banking to realise we're a quality outfit. They may already have some connection with the firm; father, cousin, brother, and so on. But the ones we are interested in . . . well, we'll waste no time letting them know they'd be on a winning wicket with us. Are we agreed?'

'Discreet, yet forceful?' suggested Tanya.

'Good girl!' He beamed at her. 'You've got the picture. Like some tea?'

With a cavalier spin of his leather executive chair, Riddle reached across his desk and punched the button on the intercom.

'Emma!' he barked. 'Tea, please!'

As if by magic, a trembling Sloane in jersey and pearls crept in with a tray of fragrant Orange Pekoe. Riddle waited until she had poured out two cups and then said, 'Emma, we'll need a cab to take us to Fenchurch Street. Have one waiting in . . . say, half an hour.'

'Yes, Mr Riddle.'

The anxious Sloane struggled out again with the tea tray.

Oliver Riddle checked the heavy gold watch on his wrist. 'We should be in Cambridge by seven, m'dear. Just time for a wash and brush up and then you'll have dinner with me at the best restaurant in town.'

'How super.' Tanya looked down bashfully into her Orange Pekoe, basking in the warmth of a munificent smile from Riddle. He had every reason to feel pleased. He had personally selected Tanya from the class of '82 and had supervised her rapid rise in the personnel department. When he first interviewed her as a final year undergraduette she had been soft-spoken and rather diffident, but she also had a magnificent pair of breasts, and it was probably for this reason that she had been selected. Riddle eyed them now, curving mountainously beneath her demure 'dressed for success' blouse, with its high neck and pussy-cat bow. Yes, Miss Tanya Dowling was shaping up nicely.

Riddle's invitation to dinner was a command rather than a request, but it never occurred to Tanya to refuse it. He had such authority, he was so . . . she groped around in her mind but could only come up with a word she had seen on the cover of bodice-ripping novelettes – masterful. From beneath her lashes she took in his appearance, the strong cleft chin, the curling dark hair, the muscular physique from seven a.m. work-outs at a prestigious City gym. His grey suit had been made by his own tailor in Savile Row and was worn with a shirt in a heavy crimson stripe and a pale yellow tie with crimson spots. On his feet were handstitched loafers in the softest leather. His clothes reinforced his authority whilst declaring to the world that Oliver Riddle was a man of breeding.

Far from being put out by his condescending manner, Tanya was flattered to have his attention. Within the bank's drearily patriarchal system, the directors were like gods who rarely even glanced at employees of a lesser status. With her heart beating a little faster than usual at the thought of two whole days with a director, Tanya stood up and walked to the door. She smiled over her shoulder and, feeling more daring than usual, ventured a saucy little wink.

'I'll see you later then . . . Oliver.'

Approximately three miles south of the City of London, in unglamorous North Lambeth, a similar scene was being enacted in the personnel department of Drummond Industries plc. Ray Doyle, Head of Personnel, was briefing his assistant; an attractive but stroppy red-head called Erica Whittie.

'Right, where were we? . . .' Ray Doyle thumbed through his grubby, biro-smeared notes while Erica yawned and stared at the ceiling.

'Um . . .' Ray took the half-burned cigarette from his mouth and sent a flurry of ash down the front of his slightly-soiled brown suit. Off the peg from Burton's, in Easy Care polyester. 'Oh, yeah, what I was going to say was we're going to have to give the little sods the hard sell. Really go for the jugular. Cambridge is going to be a hard one to crack – the snotty little buggers don't want jobs in industry. Think they're above it all. So you and I, darling—'

'Don't call me "darling",' said Erica without even looking at Ray.

'Sorry, didn't mean to . . .' Ray became flustered and dropped his papers on the floor. Bending down to pick them up, his elbow nudged a half-drunk paper cup of coffee and splattered it down his brown polyester thigh. As he rubbed at it, the vigorous movements of his torso sent a further cascade of ash tumbling down his front. Erica grimaced and looked in the other direction.

The door opened and Clive Fender, Drummond's chairman, stuck his head round the door. He was a large man of sixty or so, with white hair and a permanently bemused smile, like Santa Claus without the beard.

'Everything all right?' he asked rubbing his hands together. This did not elicit a reply. Ray was still fumbling with his notes and Erica ignored him. 'Splendid, splendid!' Fender pronounced, and disappeared.

Ray straightened up, took a deep breath and tried again. 'So – Cambridge . . .'

'I'd like some tea.' said Erica pointedly.

Ray glanced at his watch. 'It's quarter to five – Doreen should have been round by now . . .'

4

If he had hoped that this comment would appease the fiery Erica, he was wrong. She continued to stare at him, stonily.

'Er, I'll go and see what I can do.'

Lodging his cigarette in the corner of his mouth, Ray darted into the corridor and flagged down tea-lady Doreen Thwort who was pushing her trolley in the direction of the typing pool.

'Doreen, thank God! Can you do us two cups? Only I've got . . . Erica in with me.'

Doreen raised her eyebrows and tutted. 'I came by 'alf 'our ago, only Mr Fender said you was busy. Here—' She dribbled a thin stream from the urn, half filling two olive-drab earthenware cups. 'That's the best I can do. I've got The Girls to do yet.'

Ray carried the tea back to Erica, who sniffed at the amount in her cup.

'So . . . it's the hard sell.' Ray settled himself behind his desk and lit up another cigarette. 'We draw attention to Drummond's track record in the liquor industry, and highlight the takeover of the Star pharmaceutical group.'

'We haven't taken them over yet.' pointed out Erica.

'No, but we have to put on a confident front. Besides, Fender says we're almost home and dry now. All over bar the handshake.'

'I'm sure the head of Rapier Industries doesn't see it that way. Their bid's got an even chance, I'd say.'

Ray was about to reprimand Erica for being disloyal to the company, but thought better of it. Instead he stubbed out his cigarette and slammed his hands face down on the desk with what he hoped was positive and masterful body language.

'So . . . another couple of hours and we'll be living it up in Cambridge. How about you and me taking the opportunity to get a bit better acquainted?'

Erica stared at him. 'What?'

'I said . . .' Suddenly nervous, Ray fumbled for his fags. 'How about having dinner with me tonight?'

An expression crossed Erica's face that was half laugh, half retch. 'With you?' Girding herself with her leather shoulder bag, she strode to the door.

' . . . You must really think I'm desperate.'

Doing 'The Girls' was the high point of Doreen Thwort's day.

The sound of her trolley, rattling its way into the typing pool was always met by high-pitched shrieks of welcome.

'Look who it is, girls!' shouted Sandra, the loud-mouth of the group. 'The Angie Watts of Drummond Industries, gracing us with her company!'

'Hilda Ogden, more like!' said Debbie, the youngest.

Doreen grinned and chuckled as she poured them their tea. They always liked to tease her a bit, that was their way of showing her they liked her. They were a noisy lot who enjoyed nothing better than to take the mickey.

'Here – haven't you got something a bit stronger?' asked Sandra as she took her tea. 'I feel more like a double gin, I can tell you, after doing his bleeding nib's memos!'

Doreen leaned against the edge of a desk and eased her small, fat feet out of the plastic sandals she wore at work. The typing pool was a place where she could relax for a while, have a rest after the rigours of the executive floors. 'Oh, me bleedin' feet!'

'Here, sit down' said Carol. 'Take the weight off your bunions.'

'In a minute, I've got something to show her first!' Sandra grabbed at Doreen's elbow and led her over to the corner where her desk stood. She was a strapping, big-boned woman with heavily highlighted blonde hair and a cleavage like the Grand Canyon. 'You'll like this, Doe.'

The walls around Sandra's desk were plastered with large colour photographs which, on closer inspection turned out to be centrefolds from *Playgirl* magazine. Beefy, suntanned young men grinned out ingenuously at the members of the typing pool, their members covered by sellotaped-on scraps of paper. These tokens of modesty, like Adam's fig leaf, could be lifted to reveal the centre of interest beneath.

Sandra flicked one up with a long scarlet talon. 'This is the latest, Doe. What d'you reckon, eh? Get a load of his meat and two veg!'

Doreen gasped and covered her mouth. Then she gave a coarse little laugh. 'I could do with one of those to stir the tea with!'

Sandra sighed. 'Wish someone would pay me for standing around in nothing but a smile. I reckon it's an easy way to make a few quid. That's what your youngest's doing, isn't it?'

Doreen glowed with pride at the mention of her youngest daughter, twenty-year-old Sammi-Dawn. 'Yeah, that's right, she's doing a bit of modellin', just part time.'

'Here Doreen, you should tell her to enter this competition,' chipped in Carol, holding up her copy of the tabloid *Daily Meteor*. She brandished a double page spread illustrated by a pouting nubile dressed in skimpy lace knickers.

'Let's have a look . . .' Doreen took the paper and read out loud. ' *"This sizzling young stunner has reached the final of our Meteor Chick of The Year competition. But it's not too late to enter, so keep on sending in those pictures, girls! We're looking for curvy lovelies aged 16–19 . . ."* '

Doreen's face registered disappointment. 'That's no good, my Sammi-Dawn's twenty, she's too old.'

Sandra snorted with derision 'They'll never know! What's a few months here or there, eh? Not much when you get to my age, I can tell you . . . I say send in her picture anway. You never know.'

Doreen waved the *Meteor* at Carol. 'D'you mind, love?'

'Be my guest.'

Doreen borrowed the scissors that Sandra was using to make a paper loincloth for Mr February, and with her tongue poking out in concentration, she cut out the entry details for the Chick of the Year competition. The scrap of paper was folded carefully and slipped into the pocket of her nylon overall. She would take it home and show it to Sammi-Dawn later.

Fifty miles away in Cambridge, undergraduates Dave Jelling and Leofred Plunkett were hanging out of a window of St Godbore's college.

They were looking across Silver Street to the Royal Gardens Hotel, where there had been much coming and going in the past hour or so. First of all there had been a bus-load of beauticians arriving for a conference which featured a red vein seminar. Then several taxi cabs rolled up outside and spat out a gaggle of business men and women who had 'London' written all over them; from the Burberry macs and velvet-collared overcoats, to the briefcases and rolled up *Evening Standards*.

These harassed executives dragging their overnight bags from the back seats of taxis were milk-rounders. They toured the larger British universities on the 'milk round': a circus designed to trawl in potential management talent before the candidates took their final exams. The companies hired a hotel conference room to give a presentation full of mendacious jokiness, about what fun it was to work for them. Coffee or aperitifs would be served, depending on the budget, and American companies often required the cringeing undergraduates to wear embarassing name badges. Then the real work began. The executives took over bedrooms with the beds removed, and with the efficiency of farmers dipping sheep, worked through their interviewees. Those who made a good impression were asked back for a second interview, and if they reached the required standard of sycophancy they received the offer of a job.

'Yup, I reckon they're milkmen.' said Dave Jelling. 'And women . . .' He leaned further out of the window to get a better look. 'Christ, look at the . . . on that one.'

In the street below, Oliver Riddle was putting a protective arm around Tanya Dowling's shoulders and guiding her up the steps of the hotel.

'There's some more, look . . .'

Ray Doyle half climbed, half fell out of a taxi, dropping his suitcase in the gutter. As he planted his cigarette in the corner of his mouth and set about retrieving the case, Erica Whittie stalked past him and into the hotel.

'Have you applied for any of them?' enquired Dave, stretching himself out on the window seat, and picking up a copy of Synge's plays. 'Are you going to sell out with the rest of them?'

'I've applied to merchant banks in the City,' said Leofred. 'That's where all the money seems to be nowadays.'

'And how d'you rate your chances?'

Leofred sighed. 'Not all that well . . . I don't know, I just don't seem to have the right . . .' He looked down at his boringly neat jeans, with creases in them, and his Marks and Spencer sweater. ' . . . the right style to be a banker.'

'I thought showbiz would be more your bag.' Dave started to pick his teeth with the point of his pencil. 'You did star in a soap opera, after all. I expected you to have a crack at acting.'

Although a most unlikely candidate for a show business

career, Leofred had set off for Hollywood the previous summer in an attempt to have a less boring long vacation than was expected of him. By mistake, he had landed the part of an Oxford-educated shrink in a cheap daytime soap called *Hang-ups*. Leofred's improvisation with the script had made him a star and the show an overnight smash hit in the States. But the British network that bought the show had ditched it after the pilot and Leofred had lapsed into his old mediocrity and the obscurity of undergraduate life. He had once believed the myth that success propagates more success, but instead had discovered how quickly the bright mantle of fame became tarnished and slipped off . . .

'What about you?' he asked Dave. 'What are you going to do?' He and Dave had been tutorial partners for two years, and they were on friendly terms, though away from their academic life they pursued separate paths. Dave didn't spend much time in St Godbore's, and the rest of his life was a mystery to Leofred. He was defiantly working class, but always seemed to have a lot of money to spend. He claimed he played in a band, and Leofred had seen him skulking around in side streets with a group of students who wore zoot suits and a decidedly criminal air.

Leofred had long since resigned himself to the fact that Dave Jelling had more street credibility than he would ever have. Today Dave was wearing faded black Levis 501s, baseball boots and a peaked cap turned round backwards so that the peak covered the nape of his neck.

'Nah,' he was saying, using his pencil to clean out his inner ear, 'I haven't applied for anything. You won't catch old Dave selling out to the system like that . . .' A faraway look came into his eye. ' . . . What I intend to do is find a way to take the system for all its worth.'

'I'm not going to do it forever,' said Leofred hastily,

anxious not to seem like an Establishment drone, 'But while there's such a killing to be made—'

'Oh, don't get me wrong, I'm not against making money. My brother taught me to study form and play the stock-market when I was a kid of thirteen or so. I just want to be an independent operator, that's all. And I've got one or two ideas about how I can do it . . .

' . . . Mind you,' he conceded, nodding in the direction of the Royal Gardens Hotel and Tanya Dowling's ample breasts. 'From what I've just seen, I'm beginning to wish I'd made some applications . . .'

In London, Leofred's sister, Heidi, was returning from work.

She turned her convertible Mercedes Sports into the entrance of the prestigious riverside complex near St Katherine's Dock and waited the required four seconds while the computer-operated camera scanned her number plate and checked that she was a resident. Then the doors slid back and admitted her to the cavernous underground car park.

From there she climbed into a carpeted lift with laser operated security cameras and a computerised voice that told her which floor she was passing. At the end of a long day at work the prattling of this invisible automaton was extremely grating, and Heidi scowled into the two-way mirrors. '*BLEEP* . . . *twenty fourth floor* . . . *BLEEEP* . . . *penthouse suite*.' The lift slid smoothly to a halt and released Heidi into a white-carpeted vestibule. She groped around in her bag, sending a shower of hair-grips, paper tissues and parking tickets onto the floor until she found what she was looking for; her remote control key.

'Stupid bloody thing . . .' she muttered. ' . . . don't

know why we can't just have Yale locks like everybody else . . .'

She pointed the electronic device at the huge double doors into the apartment. A red light flashed and the doors opened slowly. A uniformed maid stood before her, with an anticipatory smile ready on her lips.

Heidi jumped. After six months she still hadn't got used to having domestic staff.

She gave the woman a brief nod and walked past her, frowning slightly. She would have preferred to come home to an empty flat, to strip down to her underwear, put her feet up and crack open a can of beer. Instead there was a ritual to go through, certain rules to obey. The maid was now waiting for her instructions, and would hover until she had received them.

'I'll have a bath,' said Heidi with a distracted air, 'And a mineral water.'

'Very good, madam. And dinner? Shall I tell Cook to—'

'You'll have to wait for Mr Cathcart to get back, and see what he wants. I'm going out later.'

Heidi threw her briefcase onto a sofa and prowled the length of the sitting room. It was a room of unbelievable opulence. The walls were hung with original works of art measuring as much as ten square feet, and there were pieces of modern sculpture littered about, amongst Chinese opium jars, Japanese watercolours and carved African chests. One whole wall was made of glass, giving spectacular views over the marina and the Thames. At one end of the sitting room was a carpeted circular 'conversation pit' surrounded by squashy white leather sofas, and at the other a sunken whirlpool bath, beneath a mirrored ceiling and hanging greenery.

After the maid had brought in a tray with drinks on it, Heidi settled herself down in the bath to do some work.

With the bubbling water massaging her body and Vivaldi pouring from the compact disc player, Heidi went through a pile of papers, pausing occasionally to make a call on the cordless phone. After the demise of her love affair with television executive Charles Jolyon, she had abandoned her career as a researcher at TV Mayhem and found a job in Fleet Street. She was now a cub reporter at the *Daily Meteor*, tackling any assignment that the editor flung at her. Today he had told her he wanted an in-depth series on rock idols of the '80s, so Heidi was beginning the arduous series of phone calls with the rock idols' stroppy managers and agents.

A red light flashed beside the front door, telling her that someone was using their remote control key to enter the flat. That someone was her live-in lover, whizz-kid business tycoon and head of Rapier Industries, Ivo Cathcart.

He strode into the room; a square, athletic man with an astonishingly ugly red face that resembled a pig's. 'Hello, darling.'

'Hi.'

Their greetings were cursory, and neither of them really looked at the other. After six months of living together they had just reached the stage where they were able to ignore one another without there being a row afoot. The maid was instantly at his side, wanting to know her master's wishes.

'What are we going to do about dinner, darling?' Ivo shouted after he had ordered a scotch.

'I'm going out.' Heidi shouted too. The sitting room was so enormous that it was difficult to carry on a conversation with someone at its other end.

'Oh?'

'What?'

'*I just said "oh"!*'

'It's work. A press launch.

'Oh.'

Ivo lost interest. He walked over to the corner where his desk stood and switched on a computer screen. Then he opened the *Financial Times* and went through the list of share prices, comparing them with figures on the screen.

Heidi had climbed out of the bath now and she wandered over to him, dressed only in a towel. Playfully, she kissed the back of his neck.

'Hey, big-shot, feeling horny? . . .'

'That's odd . . .' said Ivo, staring at the screen.

'What *now?*' asked Heidi in what sounded dangerously like the tones of an exasperated wife.

'It's the Star takeover,' explained Ivo, without looking up, 'We're trying to acquire Star shares by offering their shareholders Rapier stock in return. Drummond are doing likewise with their shares—'

'Sounds straightforward enough.'

'It should be . . .' He checked the figures again. 'But Drummond's shares are jumping too fast . . . there's something not quite right.'

Heidi lost interest and went off into the bedroom to get ready for her press launch. Ivo kept one eye on the screen and with the other watched Heidi through the open door. With the languid and slightly bored movements of someone used to having a lot of choice, she flung open the wardrobe and thumbed through the racks of clothes that had been cleaned and sorted by the maid. She picked out a chic black Anthony Price suit and shrugged it on over black stockings and a black lace teddy.

Ivo watched her toilet closely, but felt more dispirited than aroused. In the brief months that they had been together, Heidi had changed so much, almost past recognition. When they met she had been a scruffy, independent, rebellious *girl*. Her girliness, her punkiness, her penury and her vulnerability had all inflamed his lust. Now, at twenty-six she was becoming as prematurely middle-aged as the rest of her generation; a level-headed, materialistic yuppie. And he had only himself to blame. It was he who had filled her purse with credit cards and put designer clothes on her back. He had bought her.

Heidi teetered out of the bedroom in black stilettos, a leather clutch bag under her arm. She gave Ivo a passionless kiss on the cheek. 'Bye. See you later.'

As she wafted off in a cloud of Armani perfume, Ivo made his disconsolate way into the bedroom.

Then he smiled.

Heidi had left a tide of destruction and dishevellment in her wake. The wet bath towel sat in a soggy heap on the rumpled bedspread. Bottles and brushes had been left on the floor tangled in her underwear and there was a splodge of foundation on the glass top of the dresser. One thing that hadn't changed was Heidi's untidiness.

Ivo reached down and picked up a pair of cotton bikini knickers. He lay down on the bed and draped them over his face, covering his nose and mouth. Then, with eyes firmly closed, he inhaled the stuff of fantasy.

At Drummond Industries, tea-lady Doreen Thwort was finishing her day's work. She scrubbed down her tea urn with hot, soapy water and stacked the clean cups on the trolley ready for the next day's round. Then she exchanged her nylon overall for a blue raincoat and her sandals for a pair of beige vinyl lace-ups. Picking up her tote bag, she trudged down the corridor towards the back entrance of the building. The office workers had long since left and the block was silent.

Doreen left the offices behind and crossed the yard of the factory where Drummond's gin was distilled. The bitter-sweet scent of juniper was just discernible in the air, mingling with the traffic fumes from Kennington Road. After a twenty minute wait, a number 55 bus arrived to spirit her to Plumstead Common.

Doreen's work was not quite over for the day. She had the responsibility of providing tea for her family; the two of her five children who still lived at home, her retired husband and her mother.

'Beefburgers . . .' she mused to herself as she disembarked in the High Street. Then she remembered that they had beefburgers yesterday. She liked to ring the changes and give her family a varied diet, so she decided on fish and chips.

The pubs had not long been open, and in the Marine Fresh Bar in Griffin Road, trade was slow. Big Ern, the proprietor shuffled the chips with his scoop in a desultory fashion.

'Evenin', Doreen. Cod and a medium for all your lot, is it?'

'Please, Ern.'

In one corner, a boily youth of about seventeen was cramming ten pence pieces in a fruit machine, and thumping it at intervals.

'We're getting a new one of them in next week.' Ern informed him.

'Oh yeah?' The boy went on feeding in money. 'What sort?'

'A better one.'

'Great.'

Doreen stuffed the greasy paper bundle into her tote bag and set off to 32, Ingledew Road where the Thwort family were engaged in a typical evening's activities. Ex-busdriver, Ronnie, was in the kitchen with his dogs. He had taken up breeding Rottweilers as a hobby and six of them, weighing twelve stone each, were roaming the small back kitchen. They started barking at the smell of fish and chips.

'What are them dogs doing in here?' asked Doreen testily, as she exchanged her lace-ups for a pair of fluffy slippers. 'They should be out in their kennels.'

'I thought I ought to give them the benefit and let them come in,' explained Ronnie, 'On account of Tiny feeling a bit off colour.'

The animal in question, Ronnie's prize specimen, was lumbering about, giving the table legs an experimental sniff. Then he knocked the bin over.

'Well, just keep them off our tea!'

Doreen went into the sitting room, where the sound of the dogs barking blended with the strains of Motorhead. Her son, Daylon, had just bought their new single. When the song came to an end, Daylon scraped the needle across it and started it again.

'Aren't you going to say hello to your mum?'

'Hello, Mum.' Daylon lifted one buttock and broke wind noisily.

Oblivious to the thudding from the stereo, Doreen's seventy-five-year-old mother was watching Emmerdale Farm. Next to her on the sofa was Sammi-Dawn, who was trickling enough Duo-Tan into her cleaveage to cover a 38DD. Her neat, shapely legs were already a burnished orange.

'Got a beauty contest, love?' enquired Doreen.

'Miss Photogenic.' Sammi-Dawn continued with her labours. She was a woman of few words.

'I brought you this, pet.' Doreen handed over the scrap of newspaper from the *Daily Meteor*. 'You should enter.'

'Already have. My Barry entered me.'

Barry was Sammi-Dawn's obnoxious boyfriend, a bouncer in a West End nightclub.

'I see.' sniffed Doreen, hurt at having her maternal role devalued in this way. 'Well, you're too old anyhow. I've got a good mind to tell 'em.'

Daylon started the Motorhead single for the fourth time, forcing his grandmother to turn up the sound on the TV. Her face fell in disappointment as the theme tune from *Emmerdale Farm* faded into a commercial break.

'Sodding adverts . . .'

It was the season for travel agents' hype. Sun-kissed couples frolicked in the surf and bounced a beach ball to and fro. Doreen sighed covetously. 'Ahh . . . look at that, Mum . . . *Ronnie! . . .*'

Ronnie left the dogs and came into the sitting room. 'Ron, isn't it time we booked our holiday? I fancy going back to Tossa del Mar—'

'We're not havin' 'noliday.'

'Oh, Ron, you said—'

'I said we was either havin' holiday or doin' the crazy paving out front. And I'm doin' the crazy paving.'

Seeing his wife's disappointment, Ronnie added, 'Something came for you in the post this morning. One of them prize draw things. Maybe you can win 'noliday.'

Dorren ripped open the envelope that had 'WIN! WIN! WIN!' all over it and read the letter out loud.

'*Dear rs Thwort, I'm writing to tell you that you could be one of the lucky finalists in our free prize draw, and win a car worth twenty thousand pounds! Imagine the envy of your friends in – *' The standard computer letter had left a space for the relevant place name to be typed in. ' *– Plumstead. Imagine the envy of your friends,* Mrs Thwort *when that fabulous Austin Montego drives up outside* 32 Ingledew Road . . .'

Doreen gave a disappointed sniff. 'No holidays in that one . . .'

'Never mind, doll,' said Ronnie, putting his arm around her. 'When our Sammi strikes it rich, maybe she'll take you on 'noliday with 'er earnings.'

'You must be joking!' said Sammi, plastering Duo-tan on her elbows.

Doreen was in a philosophical frame of mind, and ignored this snub. 'What I want to know is, why doesn't any of it come our way? Cash, I mean. There's so much of it out there, you keep reading about it . . . So where's our share, that's what I want to know. Ronnie? . . . Ronnie!

Her husband had disappeared into the kitchen again. 'What you goin' on about, woman?' he shouted. '*Oh, bleedin' hell!*'

Doreen ran into the kitchen but it was too late. She was just in time to see a bilious Tiny regurgitate the family's tea into its newspaper wrapping.

Two

It was a cold, dark, March morning, but the staff of the Royal Gardens Hotel in Cambridge were already hard at work. Almost all the rooms were full which meant many breakfast trays to prepare: orange juice and low-fat yoghurt for the beauticians and strong coffee and a fry-up for the milk-rounders. Then there were the newspapers to deliver to the correct rooms; the *Daily Mail* and *Titbits* to the beauticians and the *Financial Times* and *Independent* to the milk-rounders.

Just such a delivery was on its way to the Emperor Suite on the top floor, where Oliver Riddle had got to work early. He was discussing strategy with his right-hand woman, the buxom Tanya.

' . . . So, m'dear, I'll kick off with the questions about background and schooling, and then you can take over and ask them about their hobbies . . .'

'Super.'

'Then, just when they think it's nice and easy, I'll go for the jugular and ask them for a resumé of corporate finance as they see it. Got that?'

'Yes, Mr Riddle.'

'Right, into the shower with you, then.'

Covering her naked body with a sheet – a token gesture of modesty, long after cause for modesty had been lost –

Tanya obediently slithered off the bed and scuttled into the bathroom.

The second after she had disappeared, there was a knock at the door.

'Your papers, sir.'

'One second . . .' Riddle stuffed various items of underwear and a pair of stilettos under the bed before striding over to the door and flinging it open with a hearty 'Morning!' As soon as he was alone again, he flicked through the *Financial Times*. A profile on the City pages caught his eye. It was about an American industrialist called Hyman Weevil who, according to this journalist ' . . . *is making waves on the U.S. stock market and hopes to expand internationally, starting with acquisitions in Britain . . .*'

'Hmmm . . .' Riddle turned to the share prices and studied form with a practised eye. There were three prices he particularly wanted to know about: Star, Rapier and Drummond.

He waited until he could hear the sound of gushing water and Tanya's girlish rendition of 'Climb Every Mountain' before he picked up the phone. Then he dialled the number of Clive Fender, chairman of Drummond Industries.

By a happy coincidence, Oliver Riddle was a non-executive director of that company, and had a vested interest in seeing that it successfully acquired the two billion pound Star pharmaceutical group. Morever, he intended to use his position in the City to help Drummond along the way. This would be done in two ways: firstly financiers of a sympathetic nature would be persuaded to buy shares in Star, feigning independent interest. Secondly the same breed of friendly financier would be persuaded to buy heavily into Drummond stock, thus increasing the value of the stock they were bidding with and making them more interesting to shareholders than the rival Rapier stock.

Oliver congratulated himself on the brilliance of this

scheme, yet he knew it would not be easy. Not only would the deals have to be carried out secretly, privately, but also very slowly. The net would have to be tightened very gradually, well in advance of the takeover deadline, so as not to create a stir with untoward market activity.

'Slowly, slowly catches rake-off . . .' Oliver muttered to himself. ' . . . oh, hello, Clive? Riddle here. You alone? Good . . . Listen, there's an interesting possibility on the horizon . . . a four per cent block of Star shares up for grabs – want me to get one of our friendly faces dipping in to his pocket? . . . you do? . . . no, there'll be no problem . . .'

Clive Fender, a man of foam-rubber backbone, sounded nervous. In these situations, Riddle's usual ploy was to get things moving so fast the Fender didn't have time for second thoughts.

'Look, Fender, I'll have a word in the right direction, and get the eighty mill to the brokers by close today. All you have to do, old man, is to sit tight. And to make sure that my consultancy fee gets to the right account at the right time . . . Will do. I'll let you know.'

Riddle paused and reflected. What about getting in touch with Hyman Weevil, the seriously loaded American? . . . But no, the man was white trash from some God-awful southern state. He picked up the receiver and dialled again. This time it was the number of the Dorchester Hotel in London, the temporary sanctuary of nomadic financier, Demi Janus. Janus was an Armenian émigré with a billion dollar fortune to invest, and a fondness for the English.

' . . . Hello? . . . Mr Janus's suite, please . . . Good morning Demi, it's Oliver Riddle here. Just thought I'd let you know about an interesting little opportunity that's come up . . .'

Despite Janus's friendly co-operation, Riddle had broken out in a cold sweat by the time he put the phone down.

Although there were still a few months to go before the date of the Star bid, he was already putting himself in a dangerous position. Now that it was known that Star was up for sale, various bodies would be monitoring the movement of its stock very carefully. And since the financiers Riddle used were known to him socially, the risk of exposure was already high. Too high. He was in danger of making a noose for his own neck.

What was needed, he decided, was an intermediary, a third party. Someone to make contact with potential sources of funds and point them in the right direction, for a small percentage, whilst remaining anonymous, unidentifiable. Someone who would be familiar with the markets but not associated with any financial institution. Probably someone quite young, and ruthlessly ambitious . . . Money could then be moved around in large quantities without Riddle's direct involvement. And since time was of the essence. He would start looking for his Mr Fixit immediately.

Tanya came out of the bathroom, her hair brushed and her cheeks still glowing pink with the flush of decadence.

Riddle rubbed his hands when he saw her. 'You look good enough to eat, m'dear.' He gave her an avuncular pat on the bottom. 'And talking of eating, why don't you run along down stairs and get yourself some breakfast? And mind it's a decent one; none of this rabbit-food nonsense. We've got a lot of work to do today. We're going to be looking for something very special indeed . . .'

In London, Heidi Plunkett was starting her day's work. She dumped her Mercedes sports car on a vacant meter and pushed open the plate glass doors to the reception of *Meteor Newspapers Limited*. It was ten o'clock, a respectable time for a journalist to start work, and already the place was humming with activity. Uniformed commissionaires directed a flow of visitors to the twelve floors of the building, while jack-booted motorbike messengers skulked in the shadows of a bronze bust of the paper's founder, Albert Waterman. A famous topless model dressed in track-suit and dark glasses slipped into the elevator, unrecognised with her clothes on.

Heidi was headed for the editorial offices on the fifth floor. To get there she had to pass through the Pictures Department. The 'boys' who worked there were all gathered around one desk with their shirt sleeves rolled up and cigarettes clamped in the corner of their jaws. Normally they cat-called and made suggestive asides as Heidi walked past them, but this morning they were too engrossed in examining the photographs of entrants in the Chick of the Year competition.

'Blimey, Steve, look at the equipment on that one!'

'Christ, she could curtsey on my face any day of the week!'

'Take a deck at this one, lads . . . *Sammi-Dawn Thwort, aged 19, Plumstead, East London.*' She's a bit of a pouter, eh?'

'Jesus, she could pout on my—'

Then they noticed Heidi, stalking past them with her eyes fixed firmly in the middle distance, trying to pretend she wasn't listening.

One of them let out a long wolf whistle.

'Hey, Heidi, why don't you enter this competition?'

'I'm too old!' Heidi shouted over her shoulder, biting her lip to prevent herself from smiling.

'Why don't you let us be the judge of that? Tell you what, slip out of that sexy little suit of yours and we'll—'

Heidi let the swing door fall back with a crash, leaving the noisy rabble in Pictures behind her.

Joan, the editor's draconian secretary, was guarding the entrance to his lair.

'Do you have an appointment?' she asked over the top of her Edna Everage spectacles.

'I should hope so – he sent for me.'

'But—'

Heidi marched into the inner sanctum. The *Meteor's* editor, Ross Hopper, was rooting around in the fridge at the back of the room. 'Just looking for a Perrier,' he said hastily, slipping the quart bottle of Glenlivet back into his pocket. 'Sit down, sit down.'

Heidi sat awkwardly on the edge of an armchair that was placed so as to be not quite opposite, and not quite beside, Hopper.

'So, this new assignment of yours . . .'

'Rock idols of the '80s?'

'No, I want you to drop that one for the moment. I've just thought up another one.'

Hopper was a tubby man of indeterminate age with thinning red hair and execrable taste in ties. He was generally kindly and genial towards his staff, but had the great failing of expecting them to be able to read his mind.

Heidi waited for him to go on.

'The City . . .' said Hopper.

'Which city?' asked Heidi, with her customary pigheadedness.

Hopper swung his chair round so that he was looking out of the window at the sprawl of Fleet Street below. 'There are things happening in the City, everyone knows that. The question is, *what* is happening in the City? You know, when I was a lad, the place a young man headed for if he wanted fat pickings was here – in the Street. This was where you got on fast and creamed off ludicrous expenses. Now you can't see them for dust as they all race up to

Newgate and Cheapside. And the question I want you to ask yourself . . .'

Hopper swung his chair round to face Heidi again.

' . . . is, what's the catch?'

'What's the catch?'

'All that money. All that cash. They're stacked to the ceiling with cash. Six figure salaries. Can it all be made through honest graft? Is that likely?'

'I suppose not.'

'It's coined in a handy phrase: "Insider dealing". Taking unfair advantage of privileged knowledge to gain on the stock market. All you have to do is find out who, when, and where.'

'All?' Heidi's tone was indignant.

Hopper's eyes were shining. He was in the throes of a vision. 'I want the dirt, Heidi, and I reckon you're the one who can find it. I don't care what it takes. You can have unlimited expenses. Buy a bottle of champagne for each and every wide boy in the City, if that's what it takes. As long as you're in there first . . .'

Heidi knew only too well what Hopper wanted. He wanted the impossible. He wanted to take the *Daily Meteor* from being a grubby little tabloid to a pioneering organ of investigative journalism.

'So . . . you'll do it, won't you? I said to myself "Heidi will do it." . . .'

'Yes.'

To her surprise, she was even excited at the prospect. The predictable routine of her domestic life had left her feeling demoralised and lack-lustre. She needed something that would get the adrenalin flowing through her veins again.

'Good. Go to it. And remember the old motto . . .'

Heidi paused in the doorway.

'Where's there's brass, there's muck. Lots of it.'

At Drummond Industries, Doreen Thwort had been at work for hours.

She had just finished the morning round of tea and coffee and was pushing her trolley back to the sluice, when her eye was drawn by something she spotted on the company notice board. It was pinned up under the heading "RECREATION".

TO ALL EMPLOYEES:
You are cordially invited to enter the Drummond Grand Draw and win one of the following fabulous prizes:
First prize: A luxurious Daimler automatic
Second prize: A holiday for two in Antigua
Third prize: A reproduction Regency dining suite

Doreen spotted Carol from the typing pool and beckoned her over.

'Here, Carol, look at this!'

'Oooh!' Carol let out a long sigh of appreciation. 'I wouldn't half like one of them suites for my lounge/diner!'

'An' I wouldn't mind a 'noliday like that, either. Only our Ronnie says we 'ain't 'aving one this year, on account of the crazy paving.'

'Aw!' Carol made sympathetic tutting noises. ''Ere, we should enter it, Doreen. I mean, you never know . . .'

'No, I know.'

'Says here you get the application forms from Personnel . . . tell you what Doe, why don't I pop down there and get us a couple, eh?'

With a bright smile and a cheery wave, Carol clacked down the corridor in the direction of the Personnel Department.

Doreen went the other way, pushing her trolley with a spurt of renewed vigour that made the cups and saucers rattle with anticipation.

*

'Money.'

Hilary Ardent mouthed the word into the mirror and froze her lips in that position long enough to put on her lipstick.

She blotted them with a tissue and tried a different word.

'Cash. Lots of lovely *cash* . . .'

She applied a second coat.

Hilary Ardent, twenty-two-year-old undergraduate and heart-throb of St Godbore's College, was getting ready for her interview with representatives of the merchant bank, Boeler Sute. She outlined her slanting green eyes with kohl, added what beauty editors call 'lashings of mascara' and finally, for good measure, a pair of fluttery false eyelashes. Still staring fondly at her own reflection, she brushed her baby fine golden hair into a smooth bob that half-veiled her sharp little cheekbones.

Hilary was determined that she was going to be offered a job, and intended to use every weapon in her feminine armoury to make sure it happened. Her grey flannel business suit was compromised by a deep slit up the left side of the skirt, and if she crossed her left thigh over her right, the interviewer would be treated to a view of a slender, tanned thigh gripped lovingly by a black, lacey stocking top.

It did not occur to her that such sexist tactics were unworthy or degrading. Burning ambition like Hilary Ardent's has no room for such scruples. The end justified any means, however tacky, and that end was not just money, but the escape from mediocrity.

Mediocrity had dogged Hilary from the cradle, and now that she was about to burst onto the adult world she was desperate to shake it off. The world she was born into was one of suburban ordinariness. Her father was an accountant, her mother a housewife, and they lived in Purley Oaks. *Purley Oaks.* She couldn't even bring herself to say those words out loud. When someone asked her where she lived she would say 'Surrey' and hope they imagined some palatial residence overlooking the Downs. She never mentioned the run-of-the-mill girls' grammar school she had attended, and if she ever bumped into an old girl she pretended not to know them. At Cambridge she attached herself to anyone who had the faintest whiff of glamour, class or superiority about them, ditching them rapidly if it evaporated.

'Boeler Sute is the best merchant bank in London.' Hilary told her reflection. This was her way of psyching herself up – the equivalent of the footballer's pre-match chanting in the changing room. 'It pays the biggest salaries and offers the greatest opportunities. I'm going to live in the smartest part of London and meet the richest men. And nothing I do is going to be the least bit ordinary or middle class.'

The thought of her quest was like the junkie's anticipation of a high. Her eyes shone and her cheeks glowed. Satisfied that she was in a winning frame of mind, she left her room and set off on the short journey across the quadrangle of St Godbore's, through the lodge, along Silver Street and finally into the Royal Gardens Hotel, where her fate was to be decided.

'Hullo, Hilary.'

'What? . . . oh, hello.'

Distracted, Hilary stared at the owner of the voice, then remembered that he was Leofred Plunkett. She had once, briefly, been interested in him when he spent a summer vacation starring in an American soap opera, but when he lapsed into a dangerous level of mediocrity she had dropped him from her repertoire of friends.

He now merited no more than a cursory smile before she walked straight past and forgot he existed. All she was prepared to think about was making an unforgettable entrance to Room 106, where the interview was to be held.

Hilary could not hide her disappointment when the door of the hotel room was opened by a young woman.

'Oh.' she said coldly, and frowned.

The woman, who wore a velvet Alice band on her baby-blonde hair, smiled apologetically. 'Mr Riddle will be along in a moment; he had to take an urgent phone call . . . but we'll get started anyway.' She sat down behind the desk and smoothed her skirt nervously. ' . . . Perhaps you would like to tell me a little bit about yourself, Miss . . . er . . .' She ran her eye down the schedule, ' . . . Miss Ardent.'

A little bit was just about all that Hilary was prepared to reveal, and her answers to the questions about schooldays and hobbies were peremptory in the extreme. It was only when the door opened and a tall, handsome man came into the room, that she allowed a semblance of enthusiasm to creep into her manner.

'So, you live in Purley Oaks?' said Tanya. 'That must be super—'

'Tell me about the bank.' Hilary flung the question in Riddle's direction. She moved her legs so that her skirt rode up a little. 'How many women do you employ?'

Riddle gave an impatient little laugh. 'That's jumping the gun a little m'dear . . . now, tell us some more about yourself. Got a boyfriend have you?'

'I don't see—'

'Engaged? And what about a family? Do you hope to have children? Only, we do have to make sure, you see. Can't invest all that money to have you getting pregnant after the first year . . .'

Hilary smiled, loathing him. I'll get him, she thought. If I get the job I'll make sure he's sorry, the patronising upper class . . .

'At the moment,' she said, 'My ambition is to become a director of your bank.'

Riddle glanced at Tanya, then gave Hilary a pitying smile. 'Of course, you do, m'dear, and that's very commendable. But at the moment I'm afraid, we don't have any women directors. You see, we find . . .'

'I'll tell you what I find', said Hilary, fluttering her false eyelashes, and thinking that it was now or never 'I find that the prospect of being the bank's first woman director . . .' She crossed her left thigh over her right with dramatic effect, ' . . . makes me very excited.'

'Er . . . quite.' said Riddle. 'I think that will be all . . .'

A few yards away, at the end of the corridor, Leofred Plunkett was blundering around in a borrowed suit, looking for the room where the Boeler Sute interviews were being held. He opened one door, only to find the beautician's red vein seminar in full cry. A gaggle of white-coated, heavily made-up women were gathered around an examination couch.

'Now, ladies!' said one of them. 'Can we have a volunteer for the cauterisation treatment?

The volunteer stepped forward and lay down on the couch. She had short, fat legs, criss-crossed with red and blue lines like a Road Map of Great Britain.

'Now, ladies, we take the needle . . .'

Leofred made a hasty exit before he had a chance to find out what she was about to do with her needle. Eventually he found his way to Room 106 and floundered his way through a disastrous interview with the representatives of Boeler Sute merchant bank. They asked him a lot of bland and pleasant questions, but the more pleasant the tone of the proceedings, the greater the sinking feeling he experienced. It meant that he was failing to make an impression. They could obviously tell he knew nothing about high finance and was not suitable raw material to be moulded into a City whizz kid, and that was why they kept on asking him about the model plane he'd made in woodwork classes at school.

'Yes, well, it's been really interesting to meet you, Mr Plinkett. Hasn't it Miss Dowling? . . . You've really given us a lot to think about . . . sure we didn't know the stress-bearing factor of balsa was so high . . . look forward to meeting you again in the near future . . .'

Leofred made another hasty exit, but not hasty enough to avoid seeing Riddle and Tanya exchange glances and shake their heads. Feeling completely demoralised he trudged down the corridor again.

'Hey, you – in here!'

A door opened and a scruffy-looking man in a brown polyester suit beckoned to Leofred. There was a temporary sign pinned to the door that said DRUMMOND INDUSTRIES.

'You are a candidate, aren't you?' asked the man.

'Yes, but—'

'Well, you should be in here then, having a little chat with me.'

Ray Doyle grabbed Leofred's sleeve and pulled him into the room. There was a distinct smell of drink on his breath, and a half open bottle of Drummond's gin on the table.

'Sorry 'sonly me.' Ray took a swig from the bottle and fumbled to light a cigarette, 'My assistant should be here too, but she's gone off in a huff . . . bloody women . . . drink?'

'Look, I shouldn't really be here—'

''Sall right, doesn't matter if you're a bit early.' Ray dragged heavily on his cigarette, sending a windfall of ash down his jacket. 'We can just have a bit of a talk. D'you ever have this problem . . . with women, I mean.'

'I think you've got the wrong—'

'All I said was, I said: "Look darling, you're an attractive bird, how about you and me getting together to make a little music" – I mean, what's wrong with that?' Ray lit another cigarette without waiting for Leofred's reply. 'Silly bint tells me she's being harassed and goes back to London . . . suppose I shouldn't really be telling you this, I mean, I don't want to put you off the company or anything, not if you want to work for us . . . what's your name, by the way?'

'Leofred Plunkett. But—'

'Plunkett . . . Plunkett . . .' Ray looked down his list. 'Don't seem to have you down. Never mind, I'll just pop your name down here.'

Leofred tried unsuccessfully to explain that he wasn't on the list because he hadn't applied to Drummond Industries. He hadn't applied for any jobs in industry, for that matter. They lacked the glamour and gloss of high finance, and when he tried to picture 'working in industry' all he came up with was a vision of anonymous, drab corridors and long treks to a photocopying machine.

Ray Doyle wasn't listening to what Leofred was trying to say, or if he was, he didn't care. He just wanted a sympathetic ear to bend.

'Did I offer you a drink already, can't remember? . . . anyway, where was I? Women . . . I dunno what it is with them, I mean, you're trying to flatter them, right, make them feel attractive, and they get all offended . . . do you have that problem?' He paused to slurp on his gin, and Leofred took advantage of the second's respite. Before Ray could start talking again, he jumped to his feet and said. 'Well, it really was very nice to meet you. I'm afraid I've got to get going now . . .'

'Fair enough, fair enough. Doing the rounds I suppose . . . which college are you at by the way?'

'St Godbore's.'

Ray scrawled this information in an illegible hand. 'Fine, send the next one in, will you?'

Leofred opened the door, but did not have the heart to say that there wasn't a next one.

'Ah . . . they seem to be a little late.'

'Probably a girl . . .' Ray unscrewed the cap of the gin bottle and did not notice Leofred creeping away. 'Bloody women . . .'

Sammi-Dawn Thwort, though she didn't know it, was about to get her first big break.

It was Tuesday, and Tuesday night was Ladies night at Pyjamarama, the West End night club where her boyfriend Barry worked. It was Sammi's custom to go and hang around outside the front entrance in Piccadilly, dressed in her best disco gear, and when no-one was looking Barry would let her slip in free.

'Lookin' pretty tasty tonight darlin'!' called Barry when he saw her tottering along the darkened street wrapped in a leopard skin fun fur.

'Aw . . . these fucking shoes!' was Sammi's only reply. She bent down and rubbed her ankle, where a blister was fast developing in her brand new flourescent orange mock-crocodile courts.

She hobbled past her light-of-love and into the throbbing gloom of the night club, where the under–25s were gyrating on the dance floor and a few minor celebrities were spending a fortune on cheap champagne in the hope of being snapped for the gossip columns. Sammi leaned on the bar for a while in the hope that a free male would buy her a drink. She knew it wouldn't take long, not tonight when she was wearing her leatherette micro-crini and a fortune in fake tan. She smiled at a hopeful-looking young Iraqi, waited while he paid £5.50 for her pina colada, then walked past him without a word, sucking noisily on her straw. Her destination was a group of fellow 'models' who had put their clutchbags in a neat heap on the centre of the floor and were dancing nonchalantly round them. They mouthed the words of the record and stared at nothing in particular, seemingly hypnotised by the strobe lights.

The Iraqi looked forlornly after her, but Sammi didn't intend to waste her sympathy. He had money, so someone would dance with him eventually. They always did.

Outside, in Piccadilly, a gleaming white Bentley Continental was parked opposite the entrance to the Pyjamarama Club.

Ivo Cathcart had been sitting there for some time, watching girls go into the club. One girl in particular had caught his eye. All the girls were dressed to thrill, but this one seemed to have the edge. She had ventured into realms of tartiness that were bordering on plain tacky. When she passed under a streetlight that illuminated, briefly, the peroxide glare of her hair and the burnished glow of her bottled tan, Ivo felt his pulse quicken.

This 'cruising' was Ivo's guilty secret. He indulged in it every so often with the furtive enjoyment of a dirty old man in a skinflick. It was all Heidi's fault, he told himself, for having changed. No, that was unfair. It was his fault. He had wanted her so much that he had given no thought to what would happen when he got her. When she started living with him, all those temptingly grubby qualities had vanished, or been subverted. It was like Cinderella, only everything was the wrong way round, now. He should have kept her in a garret with only the minimum allowance and no-one to clean up after her. He wanted the stroke of midnight to change her back into a scruffy little slut, but it was too late now. So he looked at other girls, and he fantasised.

Ivo usually only looked but this evening was different. He was feeling reckless. Telling his driver to wait for him, he crossed the street and went into the club. At first sight it was unpromising. It had pretensions at chic, and many of the girls were smartly dressed. There was too much money around for the place to be really sleazy. It was simply second rate. He was about to cut his losses and go home, but then he saw her.

She was sitting at the bar with an empty cocktail glass in front of her, as a thinly veiled hint. Her expression seemed to say 'You can buy me a drink if you want, but don't expect me to look grateful.'

Ivo walked up to the bar and leaned against it casually. He feigned indifference as he weighed her up out of the corner of his eye. She was perfect. Very young; younger than he had at first thought. Her clothes were cheap and badly made, with unpressed hems and dangling threads, and her orange plastic shoes didn't fit properly.

'Would you like a drink?' he asked.

She shrugged. 'Don't mind.'

Don't mind was made to mind . . .

Ivo made sure he opened his wallet very wide when he paid, and held it under the girl's nose so that she would see the wad of fifty pound notes inside it. An excessive amount of cash was sure to impress her. She sniffed.

'What's your name?'

'Sammi-Dawn. Sammi-Dawn Thwort.'

Ivo felt a thrill of pleasure run down his spine at those squeaky East London syllables.

'Er . . . that's pretty. And what do you do, Sammi-Dawn. For a living?'

'Model.'

The conversation, if it could be called such, continued in this vein for a while. Sammi didn't talk much, which was exactly what Ivo had hoped for. He was content just to stare at the details of her face; at the thick layer of foundation and the cupid's bow of her mouth that had been painted on with a lip brush.

'Would you like a lift home?' he asked finally.

She looked less than enthusiastic.

'I've got a very . . . nice car.'

'All right. But I'll have to meet you round the corner. On account of Barry.'

'Barry?'

'M'boyfriend. He works on the door.' Her tone was exasperated, as though this fact should have been self-evident. 'Doesn't like me leaving with guys.'

Ivo waited dutifully in the car, until he heard the click-clack of stilettos on the pavement and Sammi-Dawn appeared, shivering inside her fun fur.

'This your car?' She stared accusingly at the long white limousine.

'That's why I'm sitting in it.'

Sammi settled herself in the leather seat beside Ivo and at last granted him a small smile of acknowledgment. It was the first time he had seen her smile and he was intrigued to discover that she looked quite pretty. The Bentley was having the desired effect. 'Thirty-two, Ingledew Road.' she told the chauffeur, as though he was driving a cab. 'Plumstead.' she added for good measure.

'Very good, madam.' said the chauffeur, and Sammi smiled again.

'You got a lot of money?' she asked Ivo as they sped down the Old Kent Road.

'Well . . . obviously.' He indicated their means of transport.

'You might not have,' sniffed Sammi-Dawn, worldly to the last. 'I knew a guy once, down Plumstead, and he had a Rolls Royce. But he only got it second hand and he spent all his money on it. Didn't own nothing else. No house or anything. He used to live in his car.'

'I can assure you,' said Ivo, failing to stop himself sounding patronising, 'That I've got enough cash to buy a few more of these if I wanted to.'

'How much?'

'About two hundred and fifty.'

'Two hundred and fifty . . . what, cars?—'

'Million.'

She stared at him, drawing in her breath slightly. 'When we get to my place,' she said finally, 'How about coming indoors for a coffee?'

The Bentley squeezed into a tiny parking place in Ingledew Road, and Ivo and Sammi crept up the path to the front door of number thirty-two. 'We'll have to be quiet,' Sammi explained, 'or we'll wake up Mum'n'Dad.'

'*What the . . . !*'

As the door to the sitting room opened a huge black shape appeared out of nowhere and hurled itself against Ivo, knocking him sideways. He thought at first that it might be a protective male relative, but it turned out to be a heavyweight dog.

'One of Dad's Rottweilers. He's been a bit off-colour, otherwise he'd be out in the kennels with the others.'

Ivo was loath to enquire about the strong smell coming from the corner of the room, or about the dormant figure on the couch who was snoring noisily.

'That's me brother, Daylon.' said Sammi, taking Ivo's hand and guiding him to the foot of the stairs. 'He sleeps in the lounge 'cause Nan's in his room.'

The sight of Sammi-Dawn's bedroom, lit by a tacky pink lightbulb, made Ivo draw in his breath sharply. The white melamine wardrobe was open to reveal rows of cheap, glitzy party dresses, and the floor was littered with pairs of high-heeled shoes. There was even a purple shag-pile carpet very similar to one that Heidi had once had in her bed-sit. Smiling, he examined the girlish clutter on the white and gilt melamine dressing table, the ranks of perfumes and lotions arranged in diminishing size, the donkey in a sombrero brought back from the Costa Brava.

It was only when the sight of his own pig-like reflection in the mirror caused him to turn abruptly away, that he realised Sammi-Dawn had started to undress. She was sitting on the edge of her narrow nylon-counterpaned bed, and unfastening her blouse to reveal a very considerable cleavage. She lifted her hand to her mouth to stifle a little yawn.

'No, no' said Ivo hurriedly. With a great effort of will, he averted his gaze from her lacy underwired bra. 'You don't have to do that. I just came up here to have a look.'

Sammi-Dawn frowned. 'You mean you're one of them perverts?'

'No, I just think it would be nice if we got to know a little bit more about one another.' Ivo thumbed through the wardrobe and took out a red sequinned mini dress. he examined it thoughtfully.

Sammi leaned back on the bed, looking relieved. 'You know, I could make this room really nice . . . if I had a bit of money to spend on it. You know, I could get a white carpet and one of them fitted cupboards with loovered doors—'

'Oh no,' said Ivo, shocked. 'You must promise me you won't do that! You mustn't change anything . . .

. . . it's perfect.'

★

In Cambridge, the residents of the Royal Gardens Hotel were sleeping peacefully. All except one. Oliver Riddle was about to go to a meeting.

Unwilling to arouse Tanya's suspicions, he had conducted the evening's horseplay in her room, then left her there alone with the excuse that he needed a good night's sleep before the last day's session. But when he returned to his room it was only to collect his jacket and tie and a file of papers before going out again.

With a cordial 'Good evening' to the night porter, he left the hotel foyer and crossed Silver Street. After the well-regulated warmth of the hotel the sharp frost chilled him, but he did not have far to walk. St Godbore's college was only a few yards away, and the door to the porter's lodge would be open for a few minutes yet.

Trying hard to look casual, Riddle tucked his file under his arm and sauntered across the quadrangle. It was silent, deserted, but there were still a few lights on in the buildings that faced onto the quad. The harsh metallic whine of an electric guitar was just audible from the one that housed the final year students. That was Riddle's destination. He and one of its inhabitants had some business to talk.

Three

Boeler Sute Merchant Bank, Fenchurch St, London EC3

1st April

Dear Miss Ardent,

I have great pleasure in offering you a place on our graduate entrant scheme, subject to a satisfactory outcome in your final exams.

You will be starting work in our Corporate Finance division, and we would like this to be as soon as possible after your exams are over. Miss Dowling will be contacting you about a convenient date.

Finally, may I add my personal congratulations and say how much I enjoyed meeting you in Cambridge. I look forward to welcoming you aboard in a few weeks' time.

Yours sincerely,
Oliver Riddle, Director

Boeler Sute Merchant Bank, Fenchurch Street, London EC3
1st April

Dear Mr Plunkett,

Thank you for attending our recent interview in Cambridge. I regret to inform you that we are unable to offer you a position at this point in time.

May I thank you for your interest in Boeler Sute and wish you luck with your future endeavours.

Yours sincerely,
Oliver Riddle, Director

Drummond Industries plc, Juniper House, London SE11

1st April

Dear Leofred,

It was great meeting you in Cambridge and I enjoyed our little chat. The good news is that we're prepared to offer you a position as Management Trainee. The bad news is that we're a bit short-staffed here, so we'd like you to get started as soon as possible after the end of your exams.

The lovely Erica will be in touch with the details.

Cheers,
Ray Doyle, Personnel Manager

'So, this is it.'

'Yup, this is it.'

Dave Jelling was standing at the centre of Leofred's empty college room, staring at his trunk. It was the end of May, and the last paper of their exams had just finished.

'So you're really going to take this job?' asked Dave. He was wearing a tassled leather jacket and motorbike boots that jangled as he strode around the room. 'The one in the faceless fascist corporation?'

Leofred shrugged. 'There doesn't seem to be any other option at the moment.' Aware of how feeble this sounded, he added, 'Anyway, I'm beginning to think it might really be quite interesting. The word is that Drummond might be taking over the Star Group.'

'Oh, yeah . . .' said Dave vaguely. He pulled out a packet of Woodbines and struck a match on the sole of his boot.

'What about you?' asked Leofred, 'You still haven't told me what your plans are.'

Privately, Leofred was rather worried about his friend's chances. His attitude to revision had been distinctly lackadaisical, and he had failed to turn up for one of the papers. In fact he had taken off to London 'on business' for two whole days, right in the middle of finals.

' . . . I mean, aren't you a bit, er . . . concerned? The examiners may penalise you. In fact, they'll almost definitely decide not to award you a degree at all—'

'Hey!' Dave slapped Leofred on the shoulder and grinned. 'Take it easy!' His grin turned to a mysterious smirk. 'I don't need a degree for where I'm going. Believe me, I'm going to be doing my own thing . . .'

After they had said their final goodbyes Leofred tried to imagine Dave Jelling doing 'his own thing'. Starring in an alternative comedy workshop, perhaps, or busking in a tube station . . .

His sister, Heidi, had arranged for a car to come and collect the bulk of his belongings, so when Leofred trudged across the quadrangle it was with no more than a small suitcase in his hand. It was a warm, sunny afternoon and the grass square around the sundial was thronging with students, many of them dressed in tennis clothes, some of them sunbathing on the lawn. One or two of them waved at Leofred as he passed, but none of them took much notice. They were far to engrossed in enjoying their precious last hours of studenthood.

Turning into Newnham Road and heading for the station, he felt a surge of bitter disappointment. This, as Dave had pointed out, was it, and he couldn't believe that there was so little to it. The glorious process of 'going down' from university had found its way into the literature, it was the pinnacle of farewell to gilded youth and yet here he was waiting for the 3.12 to London, with an office job to start on Monday morning, and nobody *cared*. Nobody had even noticed. A group of school children carrying clipboards ran round and round the platform in a state of over-excitement while their teacher tried to count heads. A couple of punks munched their way through a pot of instant noodles, then threw the pot onto the ground and walked off, leaving the remainder of its contents to seep out like a puddle of vomit.

At 3.50 the overdue 3.12 finally drew up, and Leofred Plunkett went down from Cambridge for the last time.

'Hello?'

'Heyyy!'

'Jay?'

'Heyy there, Heidi! What a chilling happening! It's high time we had a bit of a rap session . . .'

Pulling the phone away from her ear, Heidi frowned into the receiver. Since he had become a producer of pop videos, Jay Cathcart's phone manner had left a lot to be desired.

There was a faint burbling from the phone, still at arm's length. Heidi placed it against her ear.

'Cut the crap, Jay, I want to have a serious talk. I need your advice about something.'

'Whatever you want, that's cool. But you may have to

come over here to the studio. We're working pretty hard on this vid. just now.'

Heidi snorted with disbelief at the thought of Jay 'working'. 'This I must see. Where are you, in Wardour Street? . . . I'll get a cab over in about an hour. Bye.'

Heidi was sitting on the white carpet in her apartment, fenced in by a ring of press cuttings, scribbled notes, photocopied pages. She had been doing her homework on the City investigation and she thought she might be onto something. After ploughing through hundreds of back numbers of *Acquisitions* magazine she had noticed one name that kept recurring in connection with both Drummond and Star.

There was a rustling noise behind her. Turning, she saw the face of the maid as she lurked among the leaves of a huge rubber plant, like a hunter stalking it's prey.

'Can I get you something, madam?'

'No, I'm going out,' said Heidi shortly. She gathered up the pile of papers and stuffed them into her briefcase. Her shoes had disappeared and the maid had to join in the search, eventually finding them in the log basket. Finally she dragged a comb through her tufty hair and ran out of the front door and into the lift, drumming her fingers impatiently as the electronic voice gave its inventory of all the floors.

Heidi had intended to go through the papers again in the cab and check her facts before she confided in Jay, but the cab driver had other ideas. She always seemed to hail taxis whose drivers liked a little chat, craning their heads over their left shoulders while their vehicles savaged the wing mirrors of parked cars and terrorised little old ladies on pedestrian crossings.

'You one of them financial whizz kids then?' this driver asked as she groped around in her briefcase.

'Er . . . sort of.'

'What d'you recommend then, for an ordinary bloke like meself?'

'Sorry?'

'What d'you reckon I should invest in.'

'Gold.' said Heidi hurriedly, remembering what Ivo had told her. 'We should all be buying gold bullion.'

'Well, that's all right then.' The cab driver grinned at her. 'I've got about twelve grand's worth of the stuff indoors. Wearing some of it now, come to think of it.' He pulled open his shirt to reveal a battery of solid gold cruci-fixes, medallions and ingots, bringing the taxi into near-collision with a lamp-post.

'Lovely.' agreed Heidi.

'Here we are babe, Wardour Street . . .'

She was deposited on the pavement outside the tall narrow building that housed Rapier Promotions Incorpor-ated, one of Ivo's many companies. Her destination was the top floor studio, where Ivo's younger brother Jay was 'producing' a video for a new young band.

She spotted Jay as soon as she got out of the lift, pacing the stripped pine floorboards of the converted loft and signalling to people with his hands. A hypotrendy and arch-poseur, Jay was dressed in one of Don Johnson's cast-off pastel suits, and sported an exaggerated sun-tan. After the spectacular failure of a take-over bid in Hong Kong, Ivo had promoted him sideways from heading the Far-Eastern division to running the video company. It was a place where he could do far less harm and the milieu suited him perfectly, since it meant that he was surrounded perma-nently by good-looking, vacuous females.

He bounded over to Heidi and kissed her on both cheeks, and she returned his embrace with warmth. Jay was a vain, egocentric light-weight, but it was impossible not to like him.

'How d'you like the band?' He pointed at two schoolboys

who were strutting up and down on the stage, their designer donkey jackets and ripped jeans partly obscured by a swirling cloud of dry ice. 'I tell you, they're going to be the next Wham! But bigger.'

Heidi squinted doubtfully at the fledgeling stars and their standard cute-girl backing singers who were moving their plimsolled feet in unison. 'I'm sure they are,' she agreed. 'After all, with promotion like this, who needs talent?'

The studio was crowded with people walking to and fro with clipboards and headphones, trying to outdo one another in importance. The young director, thin as a whippet and twice as highly strung was doing his best to compensate for any lack of talent. 'Come on boys, to the camera, to the camera!' he was shouting, 'Come on, I want you mean and moody! . . . give me anger! Give me sex! . . .'

'Is there somewhere we can talk?' asked Heidi.

Jay ushered her up some steps to a minstrel's gallery with a bird's eye view of the proceedings. A miniature bar had been set up, complete with vacuous blonde barmaid.

'A Badoit, please, Pattie and . . .'

'A beer.'

They settled themselves on a pair of high stools. 'So, what's the buzz in the Street of Shame?'

'I can tell you what the buzzword is,' said Heidi. 'Cash. Who's got how much. And how. That's what I need you to help me with.'

Jay laughed. 'Me? Lady, I can hardly add up my cheque book stubs. In fact I don't even bother to do that, hence my unbelievably huge o.d. . . . Anyhow, if money's the name of the game why didn't you just ask my big brother? He's the one with half a bill.'

For Jay, this was quite an astute observation. And a valid question. Why *hadn't* she asked Ivo? After all, not only was he a big name in the world of finance, but he had a vested interest in finding out what Drummond were up to . . .

'I don't know, I . . .' Heidi turned away from Jay's questioning gaze to look at the writhing juveniles on the stage below them, strutting and grinning. How nice, she thought. How nice to be seventeen and fancy free . . .

'Things between you two love-birds cooling off?'

Heidi shrugged. 'Something like that. Let's just say we're not exactly in the first flush of passion any more. And . . . this is work, and I like to try and keep work separate.'

This was an understatement. She desperately needed to keep them separate. Ivo had bought the flat they lived in, her car, her clothes – he owned her. This investigation represented a bid for freedom; proof that she could do something without his patronage.

'Sure, that's cool,' Jay was saying, flashing a wink in the direction of the voluptuous Pattie. 'So, what can I do?'

'Demi Janus.' said Heidi. 'Does that name mean anything to you? It should do, since you know everyone.'

'Not everyone.' Jay corrected her. 'Just everyone worth knowing. Janus . . . let me see . . .'

'He's Armenian. Sixtyish. Loaded.'

Jay had taken out his bulging lizard skin Organofax and was thumbing through it. 'Janus . . .' he clicked his fingers. 'I know! He's got a son. Educated at an English public school. Bit of a lad . . . someone was talking about him the other day. Family's investing so heavily over here, they're thinking of buying a house – something like that.'

'Can you get me an introduction.'

'For you – anything.'

'Seriously, Jay—'

'Seriously, I'll do what I can.' Jay stood up and checked his gold Rolex. 'I've got to cruise off now. Business to attend to . . .'

'And skirt to chase, no doubt?'

'What – moi? Chassez la jupe? . . .'

Heidi watched him go. He sauntered back to the studio floor, but not before making a detour in pouting Pattie's direction. 'Hi!' she heard him say, 'Have you ever considered starring in a video? . . .'

A mere mile away, as the champagne cork flies, Ivo Cathcart had an assignation.

He was meeting Sammi-Dawn Thwort at the Intercontinental Hotel, where she enjoyed riding up and down in the glass elevator and parading around the foyer in the silver fox coat that he had bought her.

'Isn't it a little warm for fur?' wondered Ivo. 'After all, it's almost June.'

Sammi sniffed. 'They do it in *Dynasty*.'

After they had been from ground floor to penthouse a few times, with Sammi clinging to Ivo like an extra limb, they went to the suite that he had booked for the afternoon.

'I'm hungry.' stated Sammi, removing her shoes and stockings but keeping on the fur.

'I'll call Room Service and get some sandwiches.'

'Not sandwiches, chocolates. I fancy a box of chocs.'

Five minutes later, Ivo was on top of Sammi-Dawn perpetrating sexual intercourse while she munched away on coffee creams and hazelnut clusters. Their affair was progressing less than dazzlingly, and if he was honest with himself, Ivo would have been quite happy to skip the sex. Sammi had a well-made body which she used with all the passion of a dead cod. The maddening passivity that had spurred the chase, was a let-down at the kill. Oh, she seemed to like him well enough, or rather his cash. At first spending money on her was fun, but she was rapidly developing expensive tastes, which meant the starvation of his low-life fantasies. He wanted Sammi-Dawn in the raw, in her natural habitat.

This will have to stop, he thought, as he climaxed with the sound of caramel-chewing in his ear. 'Couldn't we go to your place one afternoon?' he pleaded.

'No privacy.' Sammi munched on, seeming not to notice that their love-making was over.

'Not even in that bedroom of yours?'

'Depends.'

'On what?'

'If my mum's out at work.'

'And what does your mother do?' Ivo yawned, and glanced at his watch.

'Tea lady.'

'Oh? How interesting.'

'She works up at Drummond's.'

Ivo sat bolt upright in the bed. 'That really *is* interesting . . . when are you going to invite me round to meet the family?'

'Here, Doreen – look at this!'

Doreen Thwort was half way round her early morning round at Drummond Industries. Her trolley was heavy with the weight of two steaming urns, a score of cups and saucers and two large tins of biscuits. She pushed it slowly to where Debbie from the Typing Pool was standing, scrutinising the company notice board.

'Look – "*Drummond Prize Draw: Winners will be announced by Mr Fender in the Functions Room, 3pm.*" Didn't you enter that, Doe?'

'Yeah, I wanted to win 'noliday.' Doreen sounded gloomy. 'But I won't have won, I know it. I never win nothink in raffles. Except once I won a bottle of Sanatogen and a set of raffia tablemats at a works outing.'

'Awww, Doreen! You never know! You'd better go along and see, anyway. Me and the girls'll all be there . . .'

''Ere, look at that, will you?' Doreen nudged Debbie and pointed. At the other end of the corridor, a mournful Leofred Plunkett was being shown around by Ray Doyle.

'That must be the new boy,' said Debbie. 'Julie in Personnel said they had one starting today. A graduate.'

'Poor little bugger.' said Doreen.

' . . . And this is the coffee machine,' Ray Doyle was saying. 'Should you fancy a little refreshment in between the good Doreen's rounds . . . It's quite simple really, an idiot could operate it. You just put your ten pence in the top here . . .'

Forcing back a yawn, Leofred feigned wide-eyed interest in the workings of the coffee machine.

' . . . And then bingo, your piping hot liquid drops out here . . .'

Ray dropped a coin into the top of the machine and waited. Nothing happened.

'Well . . . looks like the bloody thing's broken. Usually is. Thank God for Doreen, that's what I say. Now, let me show you how the photocopier works . . .'

Leofred trudged the corridors in a cloud of Ray's cigarette smoke, wondering if there was any chance of being allowed home early. He had never before realised that boredom could induce such acute misery. Accustomed to wearing jeans and shirts for as long as he could remember, he found his new wool suit chafing and restricting and, above all, too hot. The Drummond building was 'centrally air-conditioned', which meant that all the windows were sealed shut and the air had a deathly, leaden feel to it. After only a few hours Leofred had developed sweaty palms and a thumping head-ache. And to think some people endured forty years of this!

Ray led Leofred back to the office where the tour had started and sat him down at an empty desk with a pile of company brochures to read.

'This should keep you out of mischief for a while. And if you've got any problems . . . ask Erica.'

Erica Whittie was behind a desk at the other end of the room, flicking through papers and studiously ignoring both Ray and Leofred. After studying the Drummond brochures became blindingly dull, Leofred resorted to staring surreptitiously at Erica. Her thick red hair was pinned up with two tortoiseshell combs and fell over her shoulders in waves. Below the desk he could just glimpse a slender, black-stockinged ankle. His desperate, stimulation-hungry brain started to imagine what lay above. She really was rather attractive in a school-marmy way.

'Excuse me . . .'

'Yes?' she glowered at him over the top of horn-rimmed glasses.

'I was wondering . . . that is . . . do you know what I'm actually going to be *doing?*' Most of the day had passed without any mention of his future role in Drummond Industries.

'If you've got any problems,' said Erica, looking down at her work again, ' . . . ask Ray Doyle.'

A moment later, as Leofred was trying to focus his eyes on Annual Stationery Expenditure, she looked up again and said. 'Actually there is something you can do for me. Come here, will you.'

Leofred approached her desk with his hands behind his back like an anxious thirdformer.

'Here—' she thrust a sheaf of papers into his hand. 'Take these down to Typing for me.'

Leofred opened his mouth but no sound came out.

'It's on the second floor. You'll know you're there from the noise.'

Erica was right. As soon as he stepped out of the lift, he heard a loud, high-pitched noise, which turned out to be the sound of female voices engaged in hysterical laughter.

'Aye, aye,' said one of them as Leofred appeared on the threshold, 'What have we got here girls?'

A large, blonde woman stood in front of him with her hands on her hips. Her ample bust strained against the confines of her satinette blouse.

'I'm sorry, I—'

'Hear that, girls? He's sorry – already!' There were more outbursts of laughter. 'It's alright, darling, you haven't done anything . . . yet!' She gave Leofred a wink.

'Ah . . . Erica Whittie asked me to ask you if you'd do this.'

'Erica Whittie?' Sandra gave a contemptuous snort, 'That toffee-nosed little madam! . . . But don't worry, sweetheart, bring it over here . . .' She put a hand on Leofred's shoulder and led him towards her desk. 'I'll do it, for you. In future, you come to your Auntie Sandra, remember that. I'll take care of all your needs.'

A second, unsubtle wink made Leofred blush violently and prompted a chorus of sympathetic 'aaah!'s.

'Isn't he gorgeous?' said Sandra proudly, 'Let me introduce you to everyone . . . this is Debbie, this is Carol . . . You'll have to watch yourself with her, she's a married woman . . . what d'you reckon girls? I reckon we've got ourselves a bit of all right here, don't you? How old are you, darling?'

'Twenty-two.'

'Twenty-two and never been kissed, eh? . . . Come over here, I want to show you something . . .'

Sandra put her hands on Leofred's waist and guided him towards the corner of the room where the walls had been pasted with pictures of naked macho men. 'What d'you reckon to this then?' Sandra flicked up a taped on scrap of paper to reveal a set of suntanned genitalia. 'How d'you measure up, eh? Reckon you can compete with—'

'Er, look . . .' Leofred's cheeks were burning and he could feel the sweat trickling down between his shoulder blades. 'I've really got to be getting back. Erica, I mean, Miss Whittie—'

'Oh, no . . . you can't go yet! It's the company prize draw! You don't want to miss that. We're all going, aren't we girls? . . . You can come with us. Meet the gang . . .'

Leofred found himself being herded, like a lone sheep among a pack of collie dogs, to the ingloriously named Functions Room. It was a gloomy place; the tall picture windows were obscured by grimy nets and the burnt ochre carpet mottled with stains from the never-ending round of office parties.

At one end of the room there was a long table, and Clive Fender stood self-consciously behind it. His hands rested on a large metal waste-paper bin that was to serve as the 'hat' from which the winning names were drawn.

He cleared his throat and gave the assembled company a jovial Santa-like smile. 'Righty-ho . . . is everyone here?'

The employees crowded in to get a better view of the table. Leofred became aware of Sandra behind him. She was standing very close to him, and as the people around her moved, she pressed closer still. He couldn't tell whether or not it was deliberate, but her arm was pressing against his buttocks . . .

'In reverse order then . . .' Fender was saying, 'Third,

with the lovely prize of a dining room suite – Mrs Ida Clegg from Accounts!'

Cheers of applause.

' . . . The second prize, that super holiday in the Caribbean, goes to Mr Stuart Nuttall in Sales . . .'

More applause, and some cries of 'Hard luck, Doreen!'

' . . . And finally . . .' Fender gave a showman-like pause. 'The news you've all been waiting for . . . the amazing first prize of a Daimler Automatic car . . . has been won by . . .'

'*Get on with it, you silly old git!*' hissed Sandra.

' . . . Mrs Doreen Thwort, our Refreshments Manager!'

There were gasps of envy and amazement, followed by a loud thump.

'Someone get the First Aid Box, quick! Doreen's fainted!'

Hilary Ardent's first day at work was taking on an altogether different flavour.

When she arrived she was greeted by name, and asked politely if she would wait downstairs until one of the secretaries came to collect her. She sat down on a squashy, peach-coloured sofa in the plush reception area, but instead of thumbing through *Country Life* or *Interiors*, or one of the other magazines on offer, she concentrated on absorbing all the details of her surroundings. Being the new girl was not something that suited Hilary's nature, and she intended to become an old hand as soon as was humanly possible.

The steel doors of the lifts slid open and shut silently, disgorging sober-looking young men and women in quietly expensive clothes. Hilary noticed that although they would nod and smile at one another, there was no overt fraternisation, no exchange of in-humour. Everyone was very intent on the business in hand; that of making money.

Immediately inside the revolving doors to the street there was a security area, cordoned off behind a high counter. Visitors were required to give their name and contact, and obtain a badge from two security men, who spent the rest of their time watching a bank of video monitor screens. These screens gave them a bird's eye view of the area around the lift on each of the twelve floors. One of the uniformed security guards was in late middle age and the other, Hilary couldn't help noticing, was young and rather good-looking . . . in an animal sort of way.

Hilary stared at the thick cleft in his chin, at the shaved, stubbly hair at the back of his neck and his big, meaty hands and as she did so, she felt a hot flush rising through her . . .

For Hilary had a secret weakness: a lust for what is generally known as 'a bit of rough'. She disdained men of equal social standing; all they were good for was leading on and then dumping, but when she saw a hunky plumber in his overalls, or a garage mechanic who was handy with his spanners, she felt her palms grow damp. Afraid that it showed a base strain in her own breeding, Hilary never revealed this foible to anyone. When the security guard in question returned her stare, she looked quickly away.

After a few minutes a secretary arrived to take her to her first appointment, which she described as 'an informal little chat with Mr Riddle' in the same tone that one might use to promise a special treat to a child.

After Riddle had made his standard welcome speech, full of flowery phrases and fulsome promises, Hilary leaned forward a little in her chair and said sweetly, 'Why don't you show me a list of the bank's clients, plus a breakdown of turnover for the last year, and a list of proposed investments.'

'Come, come . . .' Riddle rubbed his hands together in a jovial fashion, 'No need to worry your pretty little head about things like that; that's not what we want you for. Now, how about me taking you out for a wee drinkie this evening, after work? . . . There's a very popular champagne bar just up the road . . .'

Hilary hesitated for a fraction of a second. She despised Riddle, and was not taken in by his chummy attitude. Girls like her were ultimately of little importance to him, particularly when their backgrounds were as unillustrious as hers. He would like to see her type confined strictly to the bedroom and the office. He was probably married to a Roedean-educated ex-deb.

But on the other hand, all the more reason to lead him on. It would put her in a better position to knife him in the back later.

'All right,' said Hilary, batting her eyelashes and tossing back the curtain of golden hair that dangled tantalisingly over her sharp cheekbones, 'I'll see you there after work . . . about seven?'

After that, she thoroughly enjoyed her first day at Boeler Sute. First, she was settled in at her new desk. The office was open plan, which was disappointing, but at least she was surrounded on all sides by a flotilla of adoring males, with not another woman under forty in sight. Hilary did not like the company of other women, or their competition. Then one of the directors took her for a three hour lunch at Spencer's, a traditional City restaurant where blood-red roast beef was washed down by claret in an oak-panelled dining room, and waitresses in what looked like nannies' uniforms served spotted dick and custard or rice pudding.

Hilary spent the rest of the afternoon making long distance phone calls on her new phone and flirting openly with the enamoured juniors in her department, who brought her cups of tea and filled her stationery trays for her. At six o'clock, feeling very pleased with herself, she collected her spanking new briefcase and strolled down to Reception.

The young security guard was still there, and he was staring at her.

As she walked straight past him and reached her hand out to catch the revolving door he shouted "Ere – gorgeous!'

She felt herself blushing, and hoped it didn't show. 'Are you talking to me?' she asked coldly.

'I don't see anyone else who you could call gorgeous, do you? I don't exactly count him—' he indicated his elderly colleague, who was snoring quietly in a chair. ' . . . anyway, What are you doing tonight, gorgeous?'

Hilary adopted her most outraged, haughty expression. In fact her heart was pounding with excitement, and she was only annoyed that he might be able to tell.

' . . . Only, I'm going down the roller disco, and I thought you might fancy coming along.'

Hilary's eyes were drawn to his muscular chest, that was trying to fight its way out of his ill-fitting uniform. A badge pinned to his breast pocket read 'STEVE DIBNEY – SECURITY'. Trying hard not to stare, she said: 'And what on earth makes you think that *I* would want to go to a *roller disco*.' She gave the words the same disdain that Wilde's Lady Bracknell gave to 'handbag'.

'Dunno really. I suppose I can tell you're the kind of girl who likes a bit of fun . . . know what I mean?'

Hilary did, and the thought was sending little electric shivers up and down her spine. Of course she already had a date, but she was perfectly prepared to break it. It would all be part and parcel of Riddle's humiliation.

'All right.' she told Steve, in a low voice, 'But I'm not going to be seen leaving with you, do you understand?' She looked around her furtively. 'I'll meet you at Bank tube station in half an hour . . .'

Oliver Riddle left work promptly at seven, and headed for Lansbury's bar in London Wall.

It had once been a sober, restrained establishment, with olive-drab decor and Hogarthian prints on the walls, but since the Big Bang, all that had changed. The City's high-earning, hard living cash-rich brat pack demanded a more kitsch playground, and now Lansbury's had purple neon strip lighting round a horseshoe shaped bar, and video screens displaying TOPIC, a stock prices service. A group of LIFFE dealers lounged against the bar, still dressed in the colourful blazers that they wore on the dealing floor, their trouser legs hitched up to reveal white towelling socks and slip-on shoes.

Shuddering at the sight of this barrow-boy success, Riddle went up to the bar and ordered a bottle of Vollereaux pink champagne. The girl who was serving him took her time over opening it, and Riddle drummed his finger nails on the top of the bar.

'Don't be all day about it!' he told her, as she struggled with the cork. There was a reason for his impatience. he had just spotted someone he didn't want to be seen by, and was anxious to be out of sight.

With the bottle and two glasses in his hand, he went and sat in a darkened corner, behind a group of cocaine-high dealers who were playing a game of 'shampoo spoof'. Like all playgrounds, the City was prone to popular crazes, and this latest one involved guessing the value of a hidden coin, with the loser picking up the tab for the evening's consumption of champagne. He was now out of sight, but that meant Hilary Ardent walking right past him . . . And where *was* the girl, anyway? Riddle was not used to people being late, least of all women. No doubt she was having trouble fending off all the other offers of a date.

After fifteen minutes, with half the champagne gone, Riddle decided to stand up and check that Hilary had not come in and was waiting for him at the bar. He was a tall man and would be able to scan the room.

Tall enough, also, to blow his cover. The man he had been avoiding spotted him and waved. Conrad Janus, son of financier, Demi.

'Damn!' muttered Riddle, as Janus came over and sat down uninvited. This was exactly what he had been hoping to avoid, being seen with a member of the Janus family in public. Their two names must not be associated, or the whole take-over scam would be blown. Surely Demi would have warned his son? Perhaps he had, and Conrad didn't care. He was a playboy who lived on his wits, a risk-taker. Dangerous.

'So, Ollie . . .' Conrad gave Riddle a hard slap on the back. 'How are things?' The accent was public school heavily overlaid with Eastern Europe, a combination that was rumoured to be devastating to women. As were Conrad's curly hair and glittering black eyes. he helped himself to some champagne from the second glass.

'Er . . . d'you mind old man, that glass is taken.'

Conrad grinned and his eyes sparkled. 'You're expecting someone? . . . A lady?'

'That's right, so . . . another time perhaps? Besides, want to have some fizz left when the young lady arrives—'

'I'll get you another bottle.' said Conrad obtusely.

Riddle decided to come out in the open. 'Look, your father and I have done a bit of back-scratching lately, probably not a good idea if we look as if we're running a consortium . . .'

'My father wants to talk.' said Conrad. 'In fact, he

wanted you to come down to our new place for the weekend.' he shook his head slowly. 'It's a pity . . .'

'Oh, I'm quite willing to *talk*,' said Riddle hurriedly, 'It's just that it would be better if we did it through someone else. A mutual friend . . .'

Conrad raised an eyebrow. 'You've got someone?'

'Yes, someone new actually., A bloody brilliant piece of recruiting on my part . . .' Riddle took a swig of his champagne. ' . . . Catch 'em young and greedy, that's what I say! He's very inexperienced of course, but completely safe. As far as the State's concerned, he doesn't exist, so the bastards from the Department of Trade and Industry would never flush him out, not in a thousand years.'

'Very ingenious,' Conrad complimented him smoothly. ' . . . his name?'

'Let's just call him Mr X. Here—' Riddle was anxious to get rid of Conrad. The shampoo-spoofers had finished and were looking at their neighbours with interest. And he didn't want Hilary to catch them together. Conrad was far too good-looking. He scribbled a phone number on a slip of paper and handed it over when he could be sure that no-one was looking.

'Thank you.' Conrad stood up and gave an old-fashioned bow. 'I hope she's worth it . . .'

'Of course.' replied Riddle with more smugness than was justified, and sat back to begin his long and fruitless wait for Hilary Ardent.

Four

Clive Fender was in the garden of his commuter-belt home when the telephone rang. As the take-over bid appraoched, he had become so nervous about his participation in white collar crime that he insisted Oliver Riddle contact him away from his office, where calls might be overheard.

He had the lawnmower in one hand and a large gin and tonic in the other when his second wife Marjorie (a blonde twenty years his junior as befitted his status) approached over the lawn with the cordless 'phone. 'Call for you darling . . .'

Fender sat down in a deckchair. 'Fender here.'

'Clive, it's Oliver Riddle.'

'Oh.' Fender did not try and conceal his displeasure. He would much rather Riddle didn't have any contact with him at all – in fact, he rather wished that Riddle didn't exist. The effort of keeping the dirt off his hands was beginning to eat away at him, bringing about a metamorphosis from genial, amiable company chairman to bad-tempered, paranoid neurotic.

'Don't worry,' said Riddle, sensing his mood, 'I've found something that's going to make your life a lot easier from now on. Well, it's not a something, it's a someone.'

'Who?' asked Fender suspiciously.

'Let's just call him Mr X. He's a go-between; an independent with no overt connections with the City. Operates completely anonymously, no-one'll ever find him.' There was no mistaking the sense of pride and achievement in Riddle's voice. 'Of course, you know what this means, don't you, Clive? Mr X is a bloody god-send, that's what he is! He's already finding buyers for Drummond stock left, right and centre, and he's willing to set up the purchase of that vital block of Star shares for us, the ones we need to clinch the bid. Once we've got them, we're home and dry. And no-one will ever trace the deals to us.'

'But I'll have to pay him, this Mr X . . .'

'Naturally.'

'Well how the hell do I do that?' The edginess had crept back into Fender's voice. 'Your money was always designated as a consultancy fee, but I can't go handing over large sums of cash to some unknown, or the DTI will be on to it before you can say "Insider dealing".'

'We're not talking about cash, we're talking about a little bonus, an inducement—'

'You mean a bribe.'

'Precisely. There must be some tangible assets kicking around that you can give to him. But that's up to you. Mr X will be calling you on Monday, so you've got the rest of the weekend to think about it . . .'

Clive Fender did think about it, but it wasn't until he was back at Drummond Industries on Monday morning that he came across the answer. It had been there all the time, literally under his nose. Gazing out of his office window, he caught sight of a long, gleaming shape in the car-park below. That was it, of course! What could make a more handsome gift than a brand new Daimler? . . .

His thoughts were interrupted by a brisk tap at the door, followed by a loud clattering as Doreen Thwort pushed her trolley into the room.

'The usual is it, Mr Fender? White, two sugars?'

'Yes, please . . . er, sit down, would you, Mrs Thwort. I'd like a quick word with you.'

'I expect it's about me car.' Doreen settled herself comfortably in the chair opposite Fender, smoothing down her nylon overall.

'Yes, it is, actually. You see, we—'

'Me and Ron decided we'd probably sell it. I mean, with the money we could do the crazy paving *and* have a holiday, and still have a bit of a nest egg left over. Anyway, we haven't got a garidge, and Ron says if we parked it in Ingledew Road it'd be about five minutes before someone was smashing into it and pulling the whatsit out. Still, it'd be nice to have a bit of a go in it first, maybe Ron could just drive me down to Southend or somethink—'

'You can't have the car.'

Doreen stared.

'That is, I don't mean you can't have it, I mean . . .'

Fender groped for words while trying to keep a jovial, man-of-the-people smile on his face. 'What I'm saying is, we'll save you the trouble and give you the cash instead.'

'But I *won* that car. It's mine!'

'Indeed you did, but since you can't drive . . . and since you were going to sell it anyway . . .'

'I never said it was definite.' Doreen's face took on a mulish look, 'I just said "probably". We might keep it after all, we might not, depending on how we feel. But it's up to us. Anyhow . . .' A note of suspicion crept into her voice, 'Why can't we have the car, eh?'

'Er . . . there's been a bit of a bureaucratic mix-up, I'm afraid. It seems that particular car is not available as a prize after all . . .'

'Available?' snorted Doreen. She stood up and smoothed down her overall with dignity. 'We'll see about that!'

*

Hilary Ardent had perfected that art of being cruel to men.

Ambitious and thick-skinned, she was nonetheless perfectly capable of winning the sympathies of the opposite sex. To do this she invented a soft, vulnerable underbelly that did not really exist. She told all sorts of lies about traumatic experiences that had left her scarred and defenceless. By the time she reached the end of one of these fairytales, with the welling of a tear in her foxy eyes brushed bravely away, her gullible companion would be overcome with a fierce desire to crush her to his manly breast and shelter her from the assaults of a cruel world.

She was doing precisely this when Oliver Riddle took her out for a drink in Jules Bar that evening. He had just made some fatuous remark about how she must have had a charmed life, or else must be a tough little cookie to have got where she was.

Hilary lowered her long eyelashes and stared down at her knees. 'Well . . . I have had problems . . .', she said in a faltering little voice.

'What you, m'dear? Don't believe it for a moment, pretty little thing like you. Have some more champagne.'

'It's true . . .' Hilary fidgeted with her gold charm bracelet. 'You see . . . I was . . . raped.'

'Good God! What sort of a monster—'

Hilary gave a tragic sniff. 'Well, he wasn't a monster actually, he—'

'You mean, you *knew* him?'

'He was a friend of the family. I . . . I was about sixteen, and I'd been out with some friends to a party. I was walking back by myself and I bumped into . . . this man. To get back to our house I had to walk across a big common, and he told me it wasn't safe for me to walk across it by myself and he'd come with me and see me safely home . . .'

'The bastard!' Without realising it, Riddle had reached

out and taken Hilary's small hand in his large one, cradling it protectively.

' . . . He just chatted away at first, he was very friendly, but then when we got to the darkest part of the common he tried to kiss me, and then he . . . he raped me.'

Hilary allowed a dramatic pause, looking up at Riddle's face through a curtain of golden hair.

'And presumably at that age you were still a . . . a..'

'Yes.' lied Hilary, who had lost her virginity by seducing a travelling salesman at the age of fourteen. 'But that wasn't the end of it . . .'

'You mean . . . there's more?'

'Yes . . . after a few months I realised I was pregnant.'

'Oh, no!'

'Yes, and my mother was furious with me. She wouldn't believe what really happened. She threw me out of the house . . . And then . . .' With a trembling of her pretty lower lip, Hilary reached the final outrage, '. . . I miscarried.'

There was a stunned silence as Riddle gripped her hand.

'. . . In the perfume hall at Dickens and Jones.' she added, as though this made the event far worse.

'Oh, you poor thing, I had no idea! Hearing that . . . well, it makes me want to just put my arm around you and give you a great big bear hug!'

Hilary smiled to herself as she sipped her champagne. 'But I've put all that behind me now,' she said in a bright, hard, brave-little-woman voice. 'And I am doing well at the bank, aren't I?'

'Indeed you are m'dear, very well indeed. Amazingly well, when you think of . . .' Riddle made a gesture with his hands, considering it not quite good form to refer to the incident in Dickens and Jones now that it had been so bravely consigned to the past.

Hilary pressed closer and let her shapely, black-stockinged thigh mould itself against Riddle's wool pinstripe. 'And do you think, at the end of my six months' probation period, there's a chance of my getting promotion?'

Riddle took out a large spotted handkerchief and mopped his brow. 'I think there's a very good chance indeed, if things . . . continue to go well. I could certainly put in a word.'

'Thank you.' Hilary purred.

'Er, listen . . .' Riddle's temperature rose by the second as he allowed himself to imagine showing her how a man should *really* treat a woman. 'I told my wife I was taking the last train back tonight. Why don't you and I go out and have a quiet dinner somewhere?'

'I'd love to, but . . . well, to be honest, late at night . . . I get a little bit nervous when I'm with a man I don't know very well.' The vulnerable note crept back into Hilary's voice.

'Yes, well of course I shan't push you m'dear.' Mentally Riddle was throwing a bucket of cold water over himself to dampen the embers of lust. 'And I hope that eventually we shall get to know one another better.'

Oh, we shall. I intend to find out all *about you, Mr Oliver Riddle . . .*

Congratulating herself on what was one of her best performances yet, Hilary gave him a suggestive little pout and went to spend the rest of the evening at Hackney Speedway with the earthy Steve Dibney.

Stuck next to the 'phone on Leofred's desk was a message:

'Your sister telephoned. Please ring her ASAP E. Whittie (Ms). P.S. Personal calls not allowed between the hours of 9AM and 6PM.'

Leofred had just returned to his converted broom-cupboard office after a tedious three hour management meeting. The most exciting item on the agenda had been the mystery of the disappearing paper clips.

He sat down at his desk and checked his watch. It was nearly six thirty, so he could make a phone call without fearing the wrath of the Valkyrie Erica. He dialled Heidi's home number, which was answered by the maid. She said that Miss Plunkett was out working, and would probably not be back until late. An attempt to get through the *Daily Meteor*'s switchboard also proved fruitless.

The door was flung open and Sandra from Typing stood before him, resplendent in a low-cut sequinned top and glittery body spray. Her turquoise eyeshadow had been replaced with gleaming gold, and her lips were a slick of fuschia lip-gloss. She wielded a gold leather clutch bag like Brittania's shield.

Putting her hands on her hips, Sandra feigned horror at what she saw in front of her.

'I hope you've got your bleedin' glad-rags with you, 'cos I'm not being seen dead with you dressed like that! You hadn't forgotten about tonight, had you?'

'No,' said Leofred truthfully. He hadn't had a chance to. For days now the members of the Typing Pool had been reminding him that he was Guest of Honour at their monthly Girls' Night Out. This was one of the many privileges that had been showered on him since that first day at Drummonds when the Girls had taken him into their care, and it was the one that made him the most uncomfortable. Somehow within the bounds of Juniper House such friendliness could be put in its proper perspective, but once they were in that cosy Lebanese restaurant, awash with cheap plonk, things could easily get out of control.

In the company of Sandra, Debbie, Carol and Jenny, Leofred left Juniper House and walked as far as South

Lambeth Road. This was in itself something of an ordeal, as the girls were in high spirits, leaning heavily on one another (and Leofred) as though they were already drunk, giggling and cat-calling at innocent workmen.

Far from being intimidated by this rabble, the patron of the Beirut Taverns welcomed them with open arms. In the past he had made many a deliberate miscalculation in their bill, when they were all too inebriated to remember whether they had ordered three carafes of rosé or five.

'Hassan, me old mate!' Sandra put her arm round him and pressed him to her bosom, an intimacy that he pretended to relish, thinking no doubt, of a hefty bill for five.

With great speed, they were shown to their table beneath a ceiling made lower by a proliferation of dangling gourds, raffia clad carafes and plastic onions bought in a clearance sale at a bankrupt French bistro.

'Bring us some of your house vino!' cried Sandra, who was always the spokesman for the group. 'And plenty of it. What shall we go for girls? Two carafes . . . three?'

Debbie pulled a face. 'Aren't we going to have a cocktail? I thought we always started with cocktails. . . .'

'God, don't get me on the banana daquiris; I'll never walk again! . . .'

'D'you remember that Happy Hour at the Blue Lagoon? When we all got a bit tiddly and started chucking the onion rings? . . .'

'And Debbie took her blouse off and started singing *Careless Whisper* . . .'

Leofred sat silently through these reminiscences, his sense of trepidation growing as a waiter arrived with glasses of coloured liquid that groaned beneath the weight of green maraschino cherries and plastic giraffes.

'Here, cheer up, sunshine!' Sandra nudged her way along the vinyl banquette so that she was pressed up close to

Leofred. 'Now, what d'you fancy?' She handed him one of the battered menus.

Leofred read through it. '*Kebabs Mediterranean Style . . . Kebabs à la Grecque . . . Spicy Kebabs . . . Doner Kebabs . . .*'

'Er . . . I think I'll probably have a kebab.'

'Good for you, that's what we're all having . . . Hassan, get over here you lazy Turk!'

'I thought we were in a Lebanese restaurant,' whispered Leofred.

'Turkish, Lebanese, same difference. They're all greasy Arabs, aren't they? Wait till you see what happens to your bowels tomorrow morning! . . .' One of the waiters approached the table and Sandra switched to a girlish smile. 'We'll have five Doners please, and some vino. And some of that funny bread stuff you do . . .'

The food eventually arrived, but only after the Girls had consumed enough wine to float a small dinghy.

'Here,' said Carol, in a conversational tone, draining her glass in one and filling it again, 'Bloody terrible about Doreen, isn't it. I couldn't believe it when I heard.'

'Shocking,' agreed Carol.

'What's happened to her?' asked Leofred, alarmed. He started to imagine all sorts of terrible accidents; runaway trolleys, exploding tea urns . . .

'Haven't you heard?' Sandra crammed a menthol cigarette into the corner of her mouth and lit it, directing the puff of smoke towards the ceiling. 'It's Doreen's Daimler, the one she won in the Prize Draw.'

'What's happened to it?' asked Leofred. 'Has someone driven a delivery truck into it?'

'No, Fender's only gone and nabbed it back, that's what, he told her she's got to take the cash instead.'

'I reckon it ought to be reported,' said Carol, 'I bet it's illegal, what he's done.'

'Tell you what though,' Sandra's eyes were gleaming. 'I bet you anything he wants that car for himself. He'll have some fancy piece he wants to give a present to, without his old lady finding out! At least . . .' She bit off a large hunk of pitta bread and chewed on it noisily. ' . . . That's what I reckon. What do you think, Leof?'

'I don't know . . .' Leofred's mind was working fast. This whiff of corruption was the first stimulating thing that had happened since he joined Drummond Industries. In any other company, the mistress theory would probably be right, but Drummond was trying to engineer a take-over. Leofred flicked through the newspaper in the company library every morning for want of anything better to do, and he had already come across several speculative articles about the bribery and corruption of the Big Bang . . .

' . . . Anyway . . .' Sandra was still talking. ' . . . We're not going to let him get away with it, are we girls? We're going to find out exactly what old Bender boy is up to. Here's to our investigation!'

The others raised their glasses in a toast.

'How will you go about it?' asked Leofred.

Sandra swelled with pride. 'We might only be lowly typists, but we get to hear a lot, believe me. Doreen's in and out of every office, and you wouldn't believe some of the phone calls she overhears. And we have access to a lot of the company business through what we type. Of course, the PSs get the juiciest bits.' She referred to the Personal Secretaries, a tribe despised by the members of the Typing Pool. 'But we can ask the cleaners to go through their bins.'

'And we can call up their stuff on the computer,' chipped in Debbie.

'That's right, the miracles of modern technology . . . If there's something going on, we'll be able to find it, don't you worry. What I want to know is, are you with us?'

'Me?' asked Leofred, taken aback. Surely they didn't

expect a newly-recruited executive to start checking up on his chairman? But on the other hand, he was yet to be given something more worthwhile to do. 'Yes, all right.'

'Great! This calls for more vino. Carol better not have any though . . .'

Carol, the mousiest member of the group, was the drunkest. Sandra, as usual, took charge. 'Someone get her a black coffee. We'd better get her sorted out – after all, she's a married woman and hubbie will be waiting for her at home.'

'What about you?' Leofred asked. He had noticed that she wore an engagement ring and a wedding band, but on her right hand.

'What me? I'm young, free and single, darling . . . well, young – maybe, free – yes, and single . . . well, I would get a divorce if I knew where my old man had got to.'

'You mean he abandoned you?'

Sandra looked coarsely. 'You could put it like that, yeah. It's such a long time ago that I can't even remember what the bastard looks like. We were only kids when we got married, stupid really . . .' She sighed into her Lebanese paint-stripper. 'We should never have done it really. But at the time I thought it would all work out, I suppose. We lived with my mum at first, spent years on the council waiting-list until we got a place of our own. We'd just got the place fixed up, paid the last instalment on the three piece suite when he buggered off. Still,' she said with satisfaction, 'I've bought private now, got me own neo-Georgian maisonette and worth every penny I scrimped and saved too.'

'Did you have children?'

'Two, boy and a girl. But they're nearly grown up now, you know how it is . . .' Sandra's voice became vague, as though she had lost interest in the subject.

'But you don't seem to regret it . . .' persisted Leofred.

'Regret it? Bloody hell, it was the best thing that could have happened to me, getting rid of my husband! I'm a single girl now, living the life of Riley. No-one to please but myself.' She gave Leofred a jolly grin, but he couldn't help feeling the perkiness was forced. 'You know what they say about single women, eh darling?'

To prove how free and fast-living she was, Sandra then suggested that they all go off to Jangles, a nearby night club. But Debbie's mother was waiting up for her, Jenny feared she already had food poisoning and Carol had to return to her husband in Bexley Heath.

'Looks like it's just you and me, sweetheart,' Sandra said to Leofred as they paid the wildly inaccurate bill and staggered out into the street.

'Er . . . I ought to be getting back soon really. There are a couple of phone calls I have to make.'

'Sawright, you don't need to make excuses. I don't mind if you don't fancy it. But I'm going to go on me own anyway. See what I can pick up. That's the excitement of being a single girl after all, eh?' She gave a self-mocking smile.

'Look, Sandra, I don't think you ought to walk about by yourself at this time . . . I don't fancy dancing, but why don't I at least walk you there? Or let me get you a cab?'

She patted his cheek. 'You're a nice bloke, you really are. A real sweetie. But no, I'll be all right. I'm old enough to look after meself . . .'

Leofred felt a pang of guilt as she set off in the direction of Jangles. He watched her go until all he could see in the darkness was the glow of her gold clutch bag, waved aloft like a torch.

Deep in the prosperous heart of the City, the drinking was still going on.

Heidi Plunkett was in Lansbury's champagne bar with Jay Cathcart and some of his friends. Getting nowhere with her inside story, Heidi had asked Jay if he could find her some likely young bloods on the receiving end of financial gossip.

The four of them sat around a corner table, beneath a video screen that was showing a Tina Turner concert. It was a warm evening and Jay was in shirt sleeves and bare feet, but Hugo – an old schoolfriend, and Gyles – whom Jay had met when he was in Hong Kong on business, kept their ties done up and their pin-striped jackets on. As they drank more and more of the pink champagne that Heidi was buying them, their faces grew redder and redder.

'It's a bit like Chinese whispers,' explained Hugo. 'Someone mentions a deal in quite a casual way, and that person passes it on, and then the next person . . . and each time the element of hysteria gets greater and sums involved get bigger.'

Satisfied with this analogy, red-faced Hugo sat back with his champagne and let red-faced Gyles take over the double act.

'In a way, the whole system is run on rumours, because rumours alone can be enough to push up a share price.'

Riddles, thought Heidi, they're talking in riddles. 'But isn't there *anything* concrete you can tell me?' she asked, ordering them more champagne in desperation, 'Have you heard anything a bit more . . . factual? And preferably something unethical, too.'

'There's a lot of talk about an American chap called Hyman Weevil. Apparently he's trying to muscle in and buy Star shares, along with everyone else. Might even put in a bid for the whole show.'

'Hardly earth-shattering news,' sighed Heidi. 'Anything else?'

Gyles looked at Hugo and Hugo looked at Gyles. Jay yawned.

'Well,' said Gyles,' there *is* a big buzz in the City right now about . . . should we tell her?'

'I don't know,' said Hugo, 'What do you think?' A natural suspicion of the tabloid press had crept into their voices, meaning they knew something worth knowing. Heidi became alert, waiting.

'Look, you've got to promise not to mention our names, okay? Only we don't want people to know we know, if you know what I mean . . .'

Heidi assured him that she did know.

'Well . . .' Gyles looked at Hugo and Hugo nodded. 'Everyone's talking about this guy called Mr X. He doesn't have another name, and no-one knows who he really is, that's the brilliant thing . . .'

'Though there are loads of rumours about who it *could* be,' interjected Hugh.

Bored, Jay plugged in his portable CD player and started looking around the crowded bar to see if he could spot anyone he knew.

'Tell me what he does,' said Heidi.

'He just introduces people to other people. He offers a service – I suppose it's like the financial equivalent of a dating agency.'

'With discretion assured?'

'Oh, absolutely, that's the whole point. Someone wants to buy, someone wants to sell, he puts them together without them having to have any contact at all. It's bloody hot stuff, I tell you. I've even heard about people bidding thousands for his telephone number!'

'And – but this is another rumour I'm afraid – I've heard that he's been involved in the movement of Star shares. Wink, wink . . .'

' . . . Nudge, nudge!'

'So, how do I get hold of him?'

'Aha!' Hugo swilled his pink champagne and dabbed his lips with a huge silk handkerchief.

'That would be telling . . .'

'Well of course it would!' snapped Heidi, who was starting to get intensely irritated by Tweedledee and Tweedledum. 'That's the whole point of this exercise! I haven't just bought fifty quids worth of champagne for the hell of it, you know.'

Hugo and Gyles looked crestfallen, like two schoolboys who've just been told a playground game wasn't all in fun after all.

'I'll tell you what,' said Gyles, after he had checked the last bottle of fizz was indeed empty. 'We can't give his phone number, because as we've said, the price of that is shooting up, but we can tell you where he lives. It's common knowledge—'

'Well, fairly common,' interjected Hugo cautiously.

' . . . that he's just bought a big house on the Bishop's Avenue with all his vast commissions. It's the one at the bottom end that's been for sale for yonks. Got ridiculous statues outside, and security gates. You can't miss it.'

'Right, let's move . . . come on Jay . . . Jay??'

Jay was staring at the entrance to the bar, with his mouth hanging open. 'Hey wow! . . . Will you look at *that!*'

A girl had just walked in, fabulously pretty, with the delicacy of fine bone china and spun gold hair. She wore a neat cream linen suit and carried a large briefcase.

Jay started to imitate the howling noise made by a dog on heat.

'For God's sake, Jay! . . . anyway, she's with someone.'

The girl was approaching a table that was already occupied by a distinguished looking middle-aged man. He stood up and kissed her cheek.

'Well, she certainly believes in keeping him waiting. That

guy's been sitting there like a total lemon for about an hour. He kept looking at his watch and, like, pretending that he wasn't . . .' A gleam came into Jay's eye. 'Look, you go on without me, okay. I'm going to go over and give her the old spiel about haven't I met her before at a party.'

'Oh Jay, you're *not!* It'll never work.'

'I bet you it will. I'll lay you a tenner.'

'Fifty!'

'Done!'

Heidi left Jay making his introductions and went out into London Wall to catch a cab to Hampstead. She persuaded the grumbling cabbie to kerbcrawl down the Bishop's Avenue until she spotted a house which had an estate agent's 'SOLD' sign outside it.

It was almost certainly the house. The huge gates were wired with every imaginable security device, and on each post there was a rearing stone griffin. The house itself was solid red brick of unremarkable post-war design, and partly screened by trees.

Heidi pressed the intercom button at the gate and pressed her lips close to it.

'Allo?' A woman's voice, foreign sounding.

'I'd like to speak to . . .' She paused. She could hardly refer to him as Mr X. ' . . . to the owner, please.'

'He's not here. There's no-one here—'

At the same time there was a clunking sound as someone else picked up a handset somewhere else in the house.

'Hello? . . . who's there?' A man's voice this time, young and unmistakably English, but otherwise very ordinary.

'There's no-one here,' repeated the woman. 'He is not here.'

'But—'

There was a muffled thud as both handsets were hung up. Heidi looked up at the house. Upstairs, there was a light in one of the windows. A partially drawn curtain was twitched, and she could just discern the silhouette of a man.

Heidi returned to her flat feeling a strange sense of excitement. Her journalistic instincts had been roused, and at least there might be some sort of article in what she had seen or heard tonight . . . *Mystery of Mister Big's Millions . . . House of Secrets . . .*

There was no sign of Ivo, which was beginning to be the norm now. The maid was not there either, and with a great sense of relief and self indulgence Heidi started undressing as soon as she walked in the door, dropping a trail of crumpled clothes through the sitting room. She dug her favourite old, balding terrycloth robe out of the back of the wardrobe and went to run herself a bath. As she lay in the hot water, sipping luxuriously from a cold can of beer, her mind was still replaying the events of the evening. There was something so provocative about the combination of the menacing stone griffins and that man's voice, so young . . .

The phone rang.

'Hi, it's Leofred.'

'Leof! How are things? How's the new place?'

Leofred had recently moved into a bedsit in Maida Vale. Heidi had pressed him to come and move in with her and Ivo, but he had preferred his independence.

'It's . . . well, you know, it's okay. No-one to bother me.'

Heidi gave a deep sigh. Perverse though it was, she envied her brother the scruffy anonymity of his little box. She often thought fondly about her old room in Queen's Park.'

'The reason I'm ringing so late,' Leofred was saying, 'Is because I've heard something that you might find interesting . . . well, I don't know. It might be nothing . . .'

More rumours, thought Heidi gloomily. She had told

Leofred about her job for the *Meteor* in the hope that he might turn mole and pass out information from Drummond.

'It's just that I think the chairman might be up to something. He appropriated a brand new car when he doesn't need one. I mean he's got one already.'

'Is that all?' asked Heidi ungraciously.

'Well, it's difficult to explain, but it just seemed a bit odd. You might want to mention it to Ivo anyway, since he's going to be bidding against us. I expect you're passing on stuff to him anyway.'

'No I am not! And I have no intention of doing so!'

As she spoke, Heidi realised for the first time that she actually wanted Ivo to lose the bid, as some sort of punishment.

'Look, I'm sorry . . . let me know if you come up with something else. Every little bit helps . . . and as for Ivo, I don't want you to tell him anything . . . Ivo Cathcart is more than capable of looking after himself.'

Ivo's evening had begun in the inauspicious surroundings of 32, Ingledew Road, Plumstead.

He had in his possession two complimentary tickets for a star-studded charity gala. There was nothing unusual about this – as one of Britain's leading businessmen he was always being invited to such functions. He didn't often attend them these days: Heidi was contemptuous of the celebrity circuit.

Sammi-Dawn, on the other hand, was dazzled by it. It was her life's ambition to parade her chest at such functions with the help of a low-cut dress. 'To further my modellin' career,' she insisted. So Ivo struck up a simple bargain with her: he would not only take her to the ball but also buy her a dress of her choice, if he could pick her up from her home and meet her family. That would give him a chance to see what inside information, if any, Mrs Thwort could give him about the climate at Drummond.

Of course he couldn't explain all this to Sammi-Dawn, and she had been stubbornly uncomprehending about his wish to go out of his way to collect her.

'You don't want to be bothered with going all the way down there,' she said. 'Why don't we just meet up West, at the Cafay de Paree, or somethink?'

Ivo wheedled as he would with a child. 'Wouldn't you rather like your neighbours to see you emerging in all your finery, and being whisked off in a chauffeur driven limousine?'

Sammi sniffed. ''Spose so.'

When Ivo arrived in Ingledew Road, Daylon was playing an electric guitar solo on a broken Squeegee mop, Ronnie was grooming the Rottweilers and Doreen was having her hair put in curlers by her mother, a long process since Doreen's mother had a bit of a tremor and she kept dropping the clips. The front room had an overwhelming smell of dog hair, vinegar and setting lotion.

'I can't make you any tea,' said Doreen in a rather surly tone. Far from welcoming the billionaire into her family she was staring at him rather suspiciously. 'Only I can't move till the curlers are done. Anyway, I expect you only drink sherry or gin and tonic, and we don't have none of that.'

Sammi took hold of Ivo's sleeve and dragged him into the cramped kitchen. 'Mum's in a bad mood,' she hissed. 'It's because of that bloody car.'

'What car?'

'The one she won at work, of course!' Sammi looked at him as if he was a half-wit. 'They gave it to her and now they're trying to take it back again.'

Ivo went back to the front room. 'Mrs Thwort, I've brought you a little gift. Just a small token in appreciation of . . . well, I'll just get it.'

He signalled to the driver outside, who at this appointed signal brought in a large gift-wrapped package. Sammi-Dawn had told Ivo that her mother's favourite indulgence was Edinburgh Rock, so he had ordered several pounds, of the finest quality, from Fortnum and Mason.

'Oooh, how lovely!' sighed Doreen when she took the lid from the box and saw the serried rows of pastel coloured sticks. 'My favourite! Look, Ronnie!'

Ronnie looked up from Nipper's toenails and grunted.

Doreen sunk her teeth into the crumbling sugar with a sigh of ecstasy. Then she brushed aside her mother's fumbling ministrations. 'Leave it, Mum, I want to have a little chat with Mr . . .' Her attention had been drawn by the gleaming white Bentley outside the window. 'Lovely motor you've got there.'

The wistfulness in her voice did not go unnoticed. 'Yes, it is a nice car, very comfortable . . . and I understand you have something of an interest in cars yourself at the moment, Mrs Thwort?'

'Well—'

'Would you like to go for a spin, and you could see the sort of things it can do?'

Doreen gazed out at the vehicle in question. Her mouth was too full of rock to answer, but she nodded vigorously.

'Splendid! No time like the present, then. If you just get your coat—'

'But you can't!' whined Sammi. 'We're supposed to be goin' out! Look at me, I'm all ready to go.'

She had spent the money he gave her on a skintight black leather mini dress. It was strapless, sleeveless and backless, and studded with rhinestones. Her fat little feet were crammed into six inch patent stilettos that made her ankles wobble and her face was aglow with shades of mauve and cerise.

'We won't be very long,' said Ivo in what he hoped was a reasonable tone. 'And since you're all ready to go, we'll be able to leave as soon as I've brought your mother back.'

'It's my hair,' said Sammi sulkily. 'I've spent hours scrunching it.' Her bright blonde locks had been whipped up into an artificially tousled mass, as though she had just crawled through a very thick hedge and had a run-in with a can of hairdressing mousse on the way. 'It'll only stay up for so long. What'm I going to do if it's all fallen down by the time we arrive?'

Ivo had no answer for this.

'And my lipstick will have bled,' she added in desperation.

'Five minutes,' promised Ivo. He waited for Doreen to cover her curlers with a headscarf and then escorted her down the path, still clutching her box of Edinburgh Rock.

'Well, this is very nice,' she said, settling herself into the back seat beside Ivo. 'Very nice indeed, I must say.' She selected a pale green stick of rock and bit into it, cocking her little finger delicately. 'Wait till I tell the girls about it at work.'

'Ah yes . . . Sammi says you work at Drummond? . . . Drink, Mrs Thwort?'

'Well now, I don't mind if I do. Do you have any of those snowball things?'

A search of the Bentley's bar turned up lemonade, but no Advocaat. Ivo substituted a shot of Crème de Menthe. 'It's called an Irish Snowball,' he told Doreen, handing her the pale green liquid.

'Mmm, delicious! . . . you know, I was going to have a car a bit like this, well, it wasn't quite as big, only then they started telling me they had to have it back, well, it's just not on is it? Specially since we, the Girls and me, reckon he's gone and given it to someone else—'

'He?'

'The chairman, Mr Fender. We reckon he's up to something.'

Ivo settled back comfortably against the leather upholstery and took a sip of scotch. 'Tell me, Mrs Thwort—'

'Call me Doreen . . . mmm, this Irish whotsit is lovely!'

'Doreen . . . what sort of a man is Clive Fender? In your opinion?'

Doreen took a moment to consider this, handling her stick of rock as if it was a cigar, and she was in a company boardroom. 'Well, now, it's funny you should say that. I mean, he's polite and friendly and that, doesn't put on airs, but . . . well, I'd say there was something a bit dodgy about him.'

'I see. Dodgy.'

'Just lately I've noticed it, he's all bad-tempered and jumpy. And I says to myself "Now what's he got to be so moody about? He's the big boss, he's got a fantastic salary, a double garage, a villa in Fuengirola. What does *he* have to worry about?" '

'What indeed?' wondered Ivo.

They returned to Ingledew Road to find that Sammi-Dawn had put her time to good use teasing her hair to new heights and applying fresh make-up. She spitefully ignored her mother's exhortation to have a good time and teetered down the front path draped in a fur coat made of innumerable tiny skins, as if hundreds of gerbil-type creatures had given their lives for it. She made sure the process of climbing into the car was as drawn-out as possible, just in case the neighbours were looking.

Several net curtains twitched, and this must have pleased her, for in a rare show of affection she squeezed Ivo's hand

and said ingenuously: 'I'm really looking forward to this, you know.'

Ivo was simply bored by the prospect but he did his best to hide it at first, pausing in the shower of popping flash-bulbs outside the Grosvenor House Hotel and exchanging a few words with the press. Beside herself with excitement, a radiant Sammi-Dawn clung tightly to his arm and grinned in the direction of each and every camera.

The event was being compèred by an ex-games show host and televised for broadcast to some bored audience at a later date. As a result all the celebrities looked as though they had been taking some euphoria-inducing drug, so anxious were they to look charming and relaxed whenever a television camera was pointed in their direction. Sammi and Ivo were seated at a round table with an ageing rock star, a newscaster and several anonymous meeja types for the duration of dinner and interminable speeches, during which even Sammi's enthusiasm started to flag.

Then there was a disco, and she really came into her own, collecting dancing partners at a furious pace. Ivo was sure that she didn't have a clue who most of them were, but she seemed to have some sort of internal radar device that not only pointed her in the direction of the best looking, most exposed men, but told her when the papa-razzi were about to grab a shot for a gossip column, so that she could fling herself into the line of fire. Ivo had never seen her smile so much, in fact she never stopped smiling. She flashed through a bewildering array of smiles as though she was posing in a photo session . . . well, she was posing in a photo session of sorts.

For a while Ivo stood around on the sidelines making business small talk and watching Sammi dance. But she never once suggested that he might dance with her, and after a while he wandered away. It gave him a chill feeling, realising that their relationship had reached its pinnacle, and what that pinnacle was. He had used her, for kicks and to get information from her mother. And she was using him, too. It should have been fair, quits, but for some reason it hurt.

Ivo wandered aimlessly into the plush gentlemen's cloakroom and sat down on a leather club chair. He untied his bow-tie, took the stud from the wing collar, which had been chafing at his thick, red neck and took off his dinner jacket. As he did so, his wallet fell out of his pocket. He picked it up and took out two photographs that he kept in there with his credit cards. One of them was an archetypal family shot; his three smiling children beneath the Christmas tree. Since his divorce from his wife Linda, he hardly ever saw them.

The other picture was of Heidi, taken on holiday in Crete. She wore a dirty singlet and a stroppy expression, and her tufty hair was stiff with sea spray and suntan oil. Ivo looked from one picture to the other and back again, and for the first time in his life he felt lonely.

Five

At ten o'clock the next morning, Jay Cathcart was still in his flat in Redcliffe Gardens.

He was sitting on the edge of his graphite designer sofa shovelling the contents of a bowl of cereal into his mouth. Shortly he would be leaving for work, but first there were a couple of important phone calls he had to make. He grabbed the receiver of his Mickey Mouse telephone and propped it between his chin and his shoulder so that he could go on eating while he dialled.

'Hilary Ardent.'

'Hi! It's Jay.'

'Who?' The voice was cold.

'Jay Cathcart. We met last night, at Lansbury's wine bar, and then I took you out for a meal.' Jay was wondering how she had managed to forget one hundred and fifty pounds' worth of dinner at Le Gavroche. ' . . . Only, we arranged to get together this evening—'

'I'm sorry, I can't make it.'

'Oh.' Jay was so unused to being refused that he could not think of anything else to say.

'I'd like to, but I've got to go to a friend's funeral,' lied Hilary.

'Hey . . . God, I'm sorry, I'm really sorry . . .'

'That's all right,' said Hilary in a brave little voice.

'Listen, I'll call you sometime . . .'

With his equilibrium deeply disturbed, Jay dialled Heidi's number.

'You owe me fifty quid,' he said through a clog of cereal.

'What?'

'Last night, at Lansbury's. You bet me fifty quid I couldn't pick that girl up. Well I did. Her name's Hilary and she works in a bank. I'm telling you, the old chat up lines are the best.'

'So what happened?'

'Well . . .' Jay shovelled more Cocoa Pops into his mouth, 'I introduced myself and we got talking and that guy she was with kept trying to freeze me out and then as soon as he got up and went into the john she just looked at me and said "Let's split" so I said "Hey, that's cool with me." '

'And?'

'Well, I was going to see her again tonight, but she couldn't make it. She's got to go to a funeral.'

Heidi snorted with laughter. 'Oh Jay! You didn't fall for *that* one, did you? Still, as you said, the old lines are the best . . .'

'Hey, look,' said Jay, suddenly impatient. 'I'm ringing you about that favour you asked me to do for you. You'd better get your bags packed, because you're going away for the weekend.'

'Jay, I haven't a clue what you're talking about.'

'I've managed to get you an invite to Demi Janus' new house for the weekend. I asked around on the old-boy grapevine until I managed to find a guy who's been invited down there for a houseparty. There is one other thing . . . only way this guy Simon could bring you along too was by saying you were his girlfriend, so don't go and blow it. And you'd better not mention your connection with Ivo, either. Don't want them to find out you're a spy for Rapier.'

'But I'm not,' said Heidi crossly.

'Okay, forget it! Just be at Ashdown Station at seven.'

Heidi left the *Meteor* offices early and went back to the apartment to prepare for her weekend away.

'I don't suppose Mr Cathcart has telephoned?' she asked the maid hopefully.

'No, madam.'

'*Damn!*' Heidi went into the bedroom and flung her shoes at the mirrored wardrobe, following it with her briefcase for good measure. Then she told herself that it was ridiculous to be disappointed by Ivo's absence. She had just committed her weekend in the cause of her investigation, so even if he had been there, she wouldn't have had time for him.

She wrenched a small, battered case from the wardrobe and started to stuff clothes in it. A diehard city-dweller, Heidi never normally ventured into the countryside, let alone spent a whole weekend there. She had no idea of the correct clothing, but settled in the end on jeans and T-shirts, throwing in a pair of grubby sneakers for good measure.

When Jay had told her to meet her escort at Ashdown station, he had omitted to say which of them was going to be collecting the other. In the end Heidi decided to take the train, on the grounds that they were supposed to be a couple and would therefore be more likely to arrive in his car.

She arrived in Kent just before seven and arranged herself in a conspicuous position in the station forecourt. For nearly half an hour, nothing happened. She was just beginning to wonder whether she should have brought the Mercedes after all, when a delapidated estate car rattled up the station approach, honking its horn. It screeched to a halt and the driver approached, waving.

Simon Derbyshire was a tall, stooped young man dressed in diarrhoea-brown corduroys. He had a bright red complexion, a distinct lack of chin and he shouted all the time.

'Hullo, there!' he bellowed, 'You must be Harriet!'

'Heidi, actually.'

'Oh well, no matter,' said Simon generously, as though Heidi had been christened by the wrong name through no fault of her own. 'Hop in.'

Heidi did her best to squeeze into the passenger seat, but the leg room was taken up by a smelly black labrador, whose nose made a beeline for her crotch.

'It's okay, she comes everywhere with me. She won't bite you, will you Queenie? Who's a lovely girl then, who's a soppy old thing?'

Simon spoke in the adoring tones some men reserve for their dogs. 'If she's bothering you, just push her away . . .'

A certain amount of small talk ensued as the car hurtled down the narrow lanes. Heidi learned that not only was Simon extremely stupid, but also his father had been an equerry to the royal family, providing his son with a circle of rich and well-connected friends. He (and his dog) spent all their time driving from country house weekends to shooting parties, thus avoiding such tedious concerns as grocery bills. He didn't appear to have a job, but presumably with such demanding friends he didn't have time for one.

'Bit of a laugh this, don't you think? our pretending to be boyfriend and girlfriend.' Simon yelled.

'Hmm,' said Heidi non-commitally, thinking '*Christ, how am I ever going to survive this? . . .*'

'Ah, here we are . . . look baby girl, daddy take you on lots of lovely walkies here, eh?'

The car had stopped outside what looked like a pair of prison gates, set in a high wall. The wall was fringed with barbed wire and patrolled by two guards in camouflage gear carrying sub-machine guns.

The labrador stuck its head out of the window and barked excitedly, its wagging rear end in Heidi's face. She thought they might shoot the beast, but they obviously recognised it, because they opened the gates and waved the car through.

'Are they planning to let us out again on Sunday?' Heidi enquired.

'Good lord, don't worry about any of *that*. That's just standard anti-terrorist stuff.'

'*Terrorists?*'

'Apparently old Janus did a few favours for the Omanis and they rewarded him with one per cent of the gross national product. Trouble is, his lot, the Armenians, don't like it very much and every now and then someone tries to lob a bomb at him. Standard sort of stuff.'

Janus's new country seat was an ugly but imposing early Georgian pile, hidden behind a screen of yew and laurel. As they entered the grand reception hall, Heidi was reminded of stately homes that were open to the public, and half expected to see cordons and signs directing her to the souvenir shop. The priceless French furniture was arranged with a chilling formality and the seats of some of the chairs were covered with cellophane. There were no personal mementos, no family clutter.

'They've only just bought the place', explained Simon. 'Still settling in, really.'

They were met by a uniformed housekeeper who made du Maurier's Mrs Danvers look positively welcoming. 'Follow me, please,' she said, as if they had hired her for an official guided tour.

They left Simon in a room on the first floor, then

continued in their cheerless procession to the top of the house, and a converted nursery that was obviously considered fitting to Heidi's status as a minor and last minute guest.

'Shall I unpack now, madam?' asked Mrs Danvers, turning down the chintz cover on the bed as though she was preparing a corpse for burial. She fixed Heidi's suitcase with a baleful stare.

'Er, no . . . I—'

'Do you wish to ride?'

'No, I don't think so—'

'It can be taken care of,' said Mrs Danvers mysteriously. 'Drinks will be served in the yellow drawing room in half an hour.' Another stare, this time directed at Heidi's creased and dusty work suit. 'You will want to wash and change.'

She was arranging something that looked like an empty pillowcase on the end of the turned-down bed.

'For your soiled underclothes,' she said, in tones of doom.

Heidi changed into jeans and a clean shirt and went downstairs at the appointed hour, but before she even got into the yellow drawing room, she knew she had done the wrong thing. Through the half open door she could see the gleam of brightly coloured silk taffeta, and the sparkle of precious stones under the chandeliers.

She turned to go upstairs and change into her suit, which was the only skirt she had, but then dismissed the idea as ridiculous. At least the clothes she had on were clean. They would just have to take her as she was.

'Hullo, darling!' boomed Simon, putting his arm around her shoulder. He added in a stage whisper *'By the way, I called you darling so they'd think we were – you know. Where's your frock?'*

'Sorry, no frock!'

'You'd better come and meet the others then.'

So this is the international jet set, thought Heidi, and a motley crew they are too . . . There was an Italian designer wearing mirror sunglasses, whose scraped-back pony tail looked as though it had had an accident with a pot of hair gel, an ageing homosexual who had been a leading light with the RSC, a couple of minor English aristocrats and their hard-faced, fair-complexioned wives. And Simon. And Simon's dog.

' . . . And this is our host.'

Demi Janus was a short, stocky man with a crumpled face and a thick east European accent. His beady little eyes looked her jeans up and down, but he seemed more interested in what was inside them.

'So – Miss Plunkett, what do you do for a living?'

'I'm in business, like yourself.'

'Are you my dear? How very interesting . . .'

The taffeta-clad matrons were staring at her over their glasses of gin and tonic. Undeterred, Heidi went on. 'I understand you're taking advantage of our booming stock market. Perhaps you'd be willing to pass on a few tips?'

'Certainly, my dear. But first, there's someone I'd like you to meet . . .'

A tall figure stepped out of the shadows, as dark and dangerously handsome as a Mills and Boon hero.

' . . . may I introduce my son, Conrad.' He pronounced it 'Konerrat'.

Shit! He's gorgeous and I'm supposed to be acting attached . . .

Conrad nodded, but said nothing, and Heidi assumed that his grasp of English was too poor. Making a concerted effort not to stare at him, she pressed on. 'Mr Janus, I'd be really grateful if you and I could get together for a little chat about investments.'

'Later, my dear, later. First, I want you to come and talk to poor Fabio.' He led her over to the thickly-gelled Italian. 'He's all alone . . .'

Heidi was sitting on Janus's left at dinner, and once again she tried to seize her chance.

'Mr Janus . . .'

Without looking up, she became aware of Conrad Janus' black eyes staring at her.

'Mr Janus, about those investments . . .'

'One moment my dear,' Janus was deep in conversation with the English rose on his right. 'I'm just telling Camilla the secret of obtaining good Wimbledon seats . . .'

To Heidi's disgust, the women were expected to take themselves off into another room, while port and stories about call-girls were circulated. They were ushered into a sitting room adjoining the dining room, and Heidi sat with her ear pressed close to the door, trying to overhear their conversation.

Most of it was maddeningly muffled, but she did catch an accented voice saying 'Excuse me, I'll just go and see where they've got to with that second bottle of port . . .'

Heidi wrenched the door open, leapt into the corridor and intercepted Demi Janus.

'Mr Janus, it's very important that I speak with you—'

'You really *are* keen, aren't you?' His beady little eyes sparkled. 'I must show you the little black book where I keep my list of useful contacts—'

'Ah – there you are, darling!' Simon appeared in the corridor and put a heavy hand on Heidi's shoulder. 'Everything all right?'

'Perhaps you would be so good as to fetch the port?' asked Janus quickly.

'Righto!'

They waited until Simon had retreated. 'Come to my room, on the first floor,' hissed Janus. 'At midnight.'

Heidi excused herself early with a fib about a head-ache, and went upstairs to her attic room. She undressed and put on her towelling bath robe, on the grounds that if she were seen wandering around, she would arouse more suspicion if she were fully clothed.

She crept down to the first floor and by a process of elimination identified Janus's room as the one behind the double doors at the centre of the corridor. As noiselessly as she could, she reached for the door handle . . .

And felt something cold and wet on her thigh.

It was a nose, and it belonged to Simon's labrador.

'I say,' he said loudly. 'On your way to my room, were you? Isn't that taking the acting a bit far?'

His surprise notwithstanding, Simon wasted no time in grabbing her from behind and shoving his hands in the front of her robe.

Heidi stamped hard on his foot. '*Piss off, will you*!' she hissed. She added in a kinder tone; 'I'll explain later.'

She crept back to Janus's room followed by the dog, who thought they were playing a game. She shut the door on its nose, and entered the room accompanied by a loud yelp.

'Is that you, my dear?' said a puzzled voice.

Janus was wearing a crimson velvet dressing gown and lying on a heavy mahogany four poster bed.

'Come here . . .' he patted the edge of the bed.

'About that black book of yours . . .'

'I haf a pain.'

'A pain? I'm sorry, I—'

Janus lifted his left arm. In the other hand he was holding a roll of elastic bandage. 'Will you bandage it please?'

Heidi wrapped the bandage around his left hand. 'Now, about that—'

'Tie it to the bed, please.'

Heidi frowned.

'Pleess, it is better that way . . .'

She unwound the end of the bandage and tied it to the post at the top of the bed.

'Now the other one.' He held up his right hand.

Heidi realised with a sinking feeling where this was leading. 'Look, I really don't—'

'Plees! I will tell you anything you want to know – anything. I will even give you the number of my wonderful Mr X—'

Heidi fell to with renewed enthusiasm, and soon Janus' wrists and ankles were attached to the four corners of the bed.

'Now, the clothes . . . in the cupboard.'

Heidi opened the wardrobe and found the grey uniform of a female SS officer, together with a cat'o'nine tails.

'I was in Berlin in the war,' explained Janus dreamily. 'And I met a wonderful little blitzmädchen. She used to punish me . . .'

'Forget it! I'm not putting that lot on!'

'Ah, but you must!'

They negotiated.

'Just the boots.' said Heidi.

'The boots and the hat!'

'All right, the boots and the hat.'

'And the whip, of course . . .'

Feeling more than a little ridiculous, Heidi pulled on the shiny stormtrooper's boots beneath her terry-towelling robe, and arranged the grey cap on her head. She picked up the whip.

There was a knock at the door and Conrad Janus came in.

'Sorry father, I didn't realise you were busy,' he said in perfect English, then turned and walked out again.

'No, wait!' Whip in hand, Heidi ran after him into the corridor. 'It's not what it looks like, honestly! We were . . . we were talking business.'

'I see.' Conrad had a faint smile on his face. 'And my father was indulging in his interrogation fantasy and getting you to whip information out of him?'

'Something like that, yes.'

'It's a pity you didn't come to me, I could have saved you the hard work. I'm the one who handles our British investments, anyway.'

He turned and strode off down the corridor.

'Wait!' Heidi strode after him in her jackboots. 'Perhaps you and I could talk about it?'

He looked her up and down, and smiled again. 'Why not. We'll go to my room.'

Shit! The most promising bit of trouser I've pulled for months and I'm going to have to shop him to the Meteor . . .

Conrad's room was as depressingly unlived in as the ground floor reception rooms, except it smelled of expensive aftershave rather than cellophane and cleaning fluid.

'I'm interested in making new investments,' began Heidi.

Conrad laughed. 'Before we go any further, you'd better take off that ridiculous stuff.'

Heidi flung the hat and the whip on the floor and sat on the edge of the bed to pull the boots off.

'Here, let me help you.'

He knelt in front of her and tugged at the heel of the boot, easing it over her calf. 'Mmmm, how firm your muscles are . . .'

His fingers traced circles on her flesh. Heidi tried to think, but the blood was rapidly emptying from her brain to her groin.

'Do you have any Drummond shares?' she groaned.

'Mmmm.' It sounded like a 'yes', but it was difficult to tell when Conrad's mouth was engaged in kissing her inner thigh.

'I don't suppose you'd like to tell me how you acquired them?' she gasped.

'Tomorrow,' murmured Conrad, his curly head rising to the level of her navel 'I'll tell you anything you want to know . . .

. . . tomorrow.'

Heidi woke at seven the next morning, feeling cold.

The sheets had been flung back and she was alone. She staggered into the bathroom. 'Conrad?'

There was no sign of him. The discarded boots and forage cap, lying where they had fallen on the carpet, were the only evidence of the night's abandonment. Heidi bundled them out of sight under the bed, put on her towelling robe and tip-toed up to her own room.

As she opened the door, she tripped over something that had been placed just in front of it; a bundle of clothes. At first she feared that it might be another selection from Demi Janus's dressing up box, but it turned out to be riding clothes, all in her exact size.

Mrs Danvers had been doing her rounds. The turned-down bed had been turned up again in a disapproving manner. Past caring, Heidi threw herself down on it and slept.

She woke at half past nine and went down to the dining room where late-comers were still eating breakfast; the two well-born ladies and Simon.

'Hullo darling!' he shouted.

Heidi glared at him, and the others looked on with

interest, assuming a lover's tiff had taken place during the night. Conrad was nowhere to be seen.

'I don't suppose you've seen Conrad Janus?' she asked Simon.

'Conrad? Yah, he's left.'

'*Left?*'

'Flew off to Monte Carlo earlier this morning. Gone to a party given by Joan Collins or something.'

I knew I shouldn't have let him put me off.! I should have pinned him down while I had the chance, before we—

'I say,' said Simon at full volume. 'Did you know you had a lovebite on your neck?'

''Ere, did you know you had a lump of scrap metal on your windowsill?'

Sammi-Dawn Thwort was paying a visit to Ivo's penthouse in St Katherine's Dock.

'It's not scrap metal, it's a priceless sculpture by Williams-Ellis! Now come over here and sit down, will you?'

Sammi draped herself on an enormous white sofa, kicked off her mock-crock stilletos and helped herself to an Elizabeth Shaw after-dinner mint from a box on the coffee table. Her penetration of Ivo's domestic stronghold was the culmination of weeks and weeks of nagging on her part, in the face of his insistence that he'd much rather be in Ingledew Road having a chat with her mother. Now that she was here, she could see that it would help her modelling career no end if she moved in. The *News of the World* could send the people from the colour supplement round and they could capture the contrast between her fake tan and the white furniture, or have her thumbing through a range of outfits in the wall to wall mirrored wardrobes.

Ivo was pacing the floor wondering why he – a practised adulterer – should feel so nervous. After all, it was only Saturday afternoon, and Heidi wasn't due back from the country until Sunday night. But somehow the fact that he and Heidi weren't married made what he was doing seem even shabbier.

'Well, now you're here,' he said to Sammi. 'How about some sex?'

'Go ahead.'

Sammi lay back and helped herself to more after dinner mints, while Ivo kneaded her breasts.

'Mmmm . . .'

'Ahhh . . .'

Chomp . . . chomp . . . '

There was an electronic buzz as the elevator arrived at the penthouse floor. The doors slid open and Heidi came in, carrying her suitcase.

'I got fed up and decided to leave early.'

Ivo had his back to her, obscuring the semi-naked Sammi from view, and at first Heidi just assumed he was reading the paper. Then he moved, exposing Sammi's best features. Heidi stared, too overcome with surprise to utter.

'Ah . . . this is Sammi-Dawn, darling. She's a model.'

'Yes, I recognise her,' said Heidi, who still hadn't seen Sammi's face. 'I've seen her . . . er, picture at the *Meteor*.'

'We were just talking, really . . .'

'Oh, I see.' Heidi's tone was calm. Her night of lust with Conrad was too fresh in her mind for her to want to lose her temper over Ivo's groping a model. However, she could not resist the temptation to be snide. 'I'd be very interested to know what you found to talk about – after all, you're nearly forty and she's just a kid of nineteen.'

'I'm twenty!' retorted Sammi, who was fed up with being referred to as if she wasn't in the room. She sat up.

'In that case you've no right to enter the Chick of the

Year competition.' said Heidi coldly. 'If I wanted to, I could have you disqualified for misrepresenting your age.'

'Look Sammi,' said Ivo, recognising the mulish look in her eye. 'I think it would be better if you went . . . now.'

Sammi picked up her fun-fur, gave a loud sniff and flounced out.

Ivo mistook Heidi's indifference for anger and set about making the situation worse.

'I didn't *want* to see her, I had to! Her mother works at Drummond and she was feeding me bits of inside information—'

Heidi stared at him for a second, then exploded with rage, flinging a priceless Japanese vase across the room so that it shattered.

'That's not *fair!* It's *my* investigation! You just want to take over everything!'

'Not everything,' said Ivo calmly. He tossed his lighter up into the air, catching it and lighting his cigarette with one smooth movement. 'Just the Star group of companies. Your life is your own affair. You're free to come and go as you choose.'

'In that case, I choose to go!'

She stormed past him into the bedroom and Ivo listened to the noises of furious packing. Then she emerged with her cases and became the second woman to flounce out on him in one afternoon.

Sammi-Dawn was hiding behind a pillar in the underground car-park, waiting for Heidi.

She watched her put her cases in the boot of her Mercedes and roar off, then she climbed back into the elevator and pressed the button marked 'PENTHOUSE'.

'D'you think she really will have me disqualified from

the competition?' she said, as an astonished Ivo opened the door.

'She might,' said Ivo. 'She's certainly capable of it. Look, Sammi—'

'Well, she's gone now, so there's nothing to stop me moving in.'

'Oh yes there is! When I said just now that I thought you should go I meant "go" – you know, for good.'

Sammi stared at him, and a very sour expression came over her face.

'Well, if you think I'm handing back that fur coat you gave me, you've got another think coming! And that gold ankle chain—'

'Keep them! Keep everything! Here—' He grabbed the box of after dinner mints from the table and thrust them into Sammi's hands. 'Keep these too!'

Sammi curled her lip and spat like a cat. 'I wouldn't have wanted to live with you anyway! Have you taken a good look in a mirror lately?. . .' She pointed an accusing finger at his red, pig-like face.

'. . . . Have you any idea how fuckin' ugly you are?'

Oliver Riddle had told his wife a lot of lies about having to work in the office on Saturday afternoon.

He was in fact at his office, but he wasn't working. He was standing in front of the full-length mirror in the executive washroom, admiring his reflection. He narrowed his eyes and ran his hand back through his thick, greying hair.

'God, have you any idea how handsome you are?' he asked his mirror image.

Then he proceeded to undress. He removed his bright red trousers (worn at weekends to convince sceptics that merchant bankers did have a sense of humour after all) and his polo shirt, and replaced them with a pair of white flannels, a pink Leander club blazer and a pink bow-tie with black spots. All that remained for him to do was tuck a fresh pink carnation in his button hole. The transformation was complete.

'Bloody dashing,' he told his reflection.

He took his discarded clothes into his office and bundled them into a drawer in his desk. On top of the desk there was a large wicker hamper, containing amongst other things, quails eggs, smoked chicken breasts, peaches in brandy and a bottle of vintage Krug. Riddle tucked the hamper under his arm and went down to the street, where his BMW was parked.

He drove up St John Street to Highbury Corner at a brisk pace, impatient of the dawdling Saturday drivers around the Angel, pulling in and out to park or collect passengers.

'Out of my way, you silly little Pakky, out of my way . . .'

Once in Highbury, he screeched to a halt outside a Regency terrace divided into flats and ran up the steps two at a time, clutching the hamper.

Hilary Ardent came to the door. She was wearing a flowered happi coat and her straight, silky hair hung lose against her cheeks. The sight of her bare legs instantly inflamed Riddle's passion, and the colour rose to his cheeks. He pulled the carnation from his buttonhole and thrust it into her hand.

She was staring at his bow-tie with a sort of disdain.

'You're not ready, then?'

'Ready?'

'I'm taking you out for a picnic, remember?' Riddle gave what he assumed was a winning smile.

'I'm afraid I'm ill.' Hilary's voice suddenly became weak and croaking. 'I've got 'flu.'

'Oh . . . I'm terribly sorry to hear that . . .' Riddle was

so used to unquestioning obedience that he couldn't help but sound amazed. 'So you won't be coming on the picnic then?'

'No, sorry'

Hilary closed the door in Riddle's face and fell back, giggling, into the arms of Steve Dibney.

'Stupid old fart!' said Steve.

He was naked apart from a pair of boxer shorts with 'Red Hot Banana' printed across the fly. Hilary tucked the pink carnation into the waistband of the shorts, pausing to consider how well Steve's hairy thighs showed them off.

'Yuk, he was wearing the most *disgusting* pink jacket!'

'I know, I had a dek through the curtains. D'you think he realised you were on the job?'

'Well if he did, he'd never dream it was with you! It would never occur to Riddle that I could be attracted to one of the Boeler Sute security guards!'

'But I know otherwise, dunn-I?' said Steve, and to prove it he crushed her in a hairy bear hug, then tossed her onto the sofa.

The telephone rang.

'Leave it!' commanded Steve, sticking his tongue so far into her right ear that it almost emerged through the left.

Hilary stretched out one arm as far as the telephone, lifted the receiver and flicked on the loud-speaking attachment. The voice at the other end was broadcast into the room.

'*Hi! Jay Cathcart here!*'

'Poncey git!' snarled Steve. 'Get rid of him.'

Hilary quite liked Jay, or at least, she liked the fact that he was the brother of a billionaire. But she cut off the call and left the receiver off the hook.

'Right,' she challenged Steve, 'Make it worth my while, you uncouth animal, you . . .'

★

At one o'clock in the morning the telephone rang, waking Leofred Plunkett from a deep sleep.

He had been dreaming about being chased down a long corridor by Erica Whittie, who was wearing vicious-looking six inch heels and wielding an over-sized kebab.

'Oi, Leof!' said the voice. 'It's Sandra!'

'Sandra? Why are you ringing me at this time of night?'

'Me and the girls are holding an emergency meeting. It's about old man Fender.'

'What about him?'

Sandra sounded excited. 'He's only done a bunk with the company money, that's what!'

Leofred tried to drag his sleep-dazed brain back from Erica's kebab. 'Are you sure?'

''Course I'm sure! You'd better come down to my place; all the others are here already.'

Leofred climbed into his clothes and caught a very slow train to the suburb of Norbury Heath, where Sandra lived on a modern housing estate. He walked to her neo-Georgian maisonette and rang the neo-Georgian door chimes.

Sandra was wearing a low-cut viscose housecoat in a shade the catalogue had described as 'maraschino cherry', high-heeled mules and full make-up. 'The others are in the lounge' she said, with a beaming smile, 'Go right on through.'

Debbie, Carol and Jennie were sitting on the sofa in various shades of coma. Leofred sank into the enveloping embrace of an old-gold dralon armchair, yawning.

'Drinkie, anyone?' asked Sandra brightly, from behind the carved wooden neo-Georgian bar. 'I think I fancy a martini, myself . . .'

Slurping on her drink, she darted out of the room and returned wheeling a hostess trolley laden with bits of food on cocktail sticks.

'Just thought I'd get a few nibbles together, in case

anyone felt hungry . . .' She passed round a plate of cheese and pineapple, then perched herself on the edge of one of the deep dralon armchairs. 'Bit of a giggle, this, isn't it?'

'Come on Sandra,' moaned Debbie, 'Get on with it! Tell us what's goin' on.'

'*Well* . . .' Sandra rearranged the folds of her cherry-red housecoat, licked a finger and smoothed it over her eyebrows. 'It's a long story, so you'll have to bear with me . . .'

Leofred tried to struggle into a sitting position but he was sucked back by the dralon cushions. He closed his eyes.

' . . . you know we were supposed to be on the look out for anything suspicious so's we could try and find out what happened to Doreen's car? Well, I just happened to mention it to Pat, on the switchboard, because she's a mate of Doreen's . . . *Anyway*, Pat was on duty this evening, and so was Alf the caretaker and he saw a light on in Fender's office and someone going in there and opening the safe. So he told Pat to call security and then he said don't bother, 'cause now I look properly I can see it's only Mr Fender. But the security people had gone up anyway, and by then Fender was nowhere to be seen, and something must have been wrong because they called their boss in. And he asked Pat if she knew Fender's home number . . .'

Sandra paused for dramatic emphasis, popping a cocktail olive into her mouth.

' . . . Anyway, they rang up and spoke to Fender's wife – of course Pat was listening in to all the calls – and she said they must have been mistaken. She said her husband couldn't have been in the office because he was away on a trip. Anyway, there was a lot of to-ing and fro-ing and it turned out that a whole load of money was missing from the safe and Fender had left the country. So Pat thought she'd ring up and tell me.'

'Well that's it then isn't it,' sighed Leofred. 'We'll never get on to him if we don't know where he is.'

'Ah, but we do!' said Sandra triumphantly. 'It's obvious, isn't it? . . .

. . . he's gone to Fuengirola!'

Six

In Juniper House, South London, the employees of Drummond Industries were preparing to go home at the end of a working day.

It had been a day of rumour and speculation, of whispered conversations outside the locked door to Clive Fender's office. But the door had remained locked and no statement had been issued, much to the frustration of the gathered media crews outside the gates. As the first whiff of scandal had leaked, they had descended on Kennington Road like a pack of dogs on the trail of a particularly smelly bone.

Ray Doyle threw his last paper dart at the bin and missed, slung his brown polyester jacket over his shoulder and left his office, knocking a full ashtray off his desk as he went. Erica Whittie put the finishing touches to a vitriolic internal memo (*Re: Sexist discrimination in the allocation of washroom space*) and locked the padlock on her Ray Doyle-proof filing cabinet.

In his cupboard of an office, Leofred put down the annual report he had been staring at for the past three hours and sighed. He looked at his watch. Six o'clock. Time to move.

He opened the door of his office and stepped into the corridor just as Doreen came into sight wheeling her trolley.

'Ah, Doreen, there you are . . .'

'Just finishing up . . .' She dropped her voice to a whisper. 'I've got you the key! Here . . .' After some fumbling around in the pocket of her nylon overall, the object in question was handed over. 'See you up there . . .'

They went their separate ways, Doreen to the end of the corridor where the elevators were, Leofred to the stairs at the opposite end. He ran up them two at a time and arrived on the executive floor just as Doreen did. She pushed her trolley along the corridor as though she was going about her rounds and Leofred strolled towards her with his hands in his pocket, trying to look casual. They converged in the middle, right outside the door to Fender's office.

'*Quick!*' hissed Doreen. 'We only got five minutes before Alf comes round to check.'

Leofred glanced over his shoulder to make sure no-one was about then turned the key in the lock. He held the door open while Doreen pushed her trolley in at full speed, cups rattling furiously, then locked the door behind them.

'What are we goin' to do?' whispered Doreen.

'The first thing to do is to check for names and addresses, phone numbers, that sort of thing. I expect his address book lives on his secretary's desk . . . no, wait a minute, what's this? . . .'

The top drawer of the desk was unlocked and there was a small green leather book in it. It appeared to be an address book, but most of the names were in code. Leofred flicked through it.

Eventually he found the heading 'Boeler Sute', but there was nothing odd about that, since Boeler Sute were Drummond's bankers. Among the initials listed, 'O.R.' had been underlined several times and had two phone numbers beside it.

'We'd better hurry up,' Doreen reminded him, 'Alf'll be along this way any minute.'

'Hang on, I just want to check his appointments' diary . . .'

At first sight it was disappointing. On Monday 23rd June there were the usual departmental meetings with Drummond staff and '5.30 – barber'. But Tuesday 24th was a different story. There was only one entry, in large letters at the top of the page – DTI. Beneath it was an arrow, implying that the meeting could go on all day.

'That's it!' said Leofred, stabbing at the page with his finger. 'That's why Fender ran off – the DTI were coming!'

'DTI – what's that then?'

'The Department of Trade and Industry! They send inspectors round when there's a takeover in the offing to check that there's no cheating going on. Fender obviously couldn't face seeing them tomorrow, which implies he had something to hide; share-supporting, that sort of thing. He's obviously done something illegal – if only we could work out what it was—'

'I know what he's done,' said Doreen grimly, 'He's knicked my bleedin' car, that's what he's done!'

An hour later, Doreen caught the 159 to Plumstead High Street and walked to the Marine Fresh Bar in Griffin Road to buy tea for the family.

'You're lookin' pretty chuffed with yourself Doreen,' observed Big Ern as he slapped five portions of haddock onto the bared breasts of a *Meteor* Page Five Chick. 'If you don't mind my saying.'

'You'd be chuffed an all if you was me' said Doreen smugly.

'Yeah, what's that then?'

'I'm only going on me 'olidays, that's all.'

'Going somewhere nice?'

'Sp—' Doreen remembered just in time that she wasn't supposed to discuss the trip with anyone. ' . . . that'd be telling, wouldn't it?'

She gave Ern a saucy wink, shoved the newspaper bundle into her tote bag and set off for 32 Ingledew Road.

The Thwort household was enjoying a rare evening of peace. Daylon was in the bathroom, painting a Union Jack on his head with red, white and blue spray paint. Sammi-Dawn – who was in the throes of a spectacular three day sulk – was locked in her bedroom with the Pet Shop Boys, shaving her armpits in preparation for a date with bouncer Barry. Doreen's mother was in the front room watching *Celebrity Squares*, and Ronnie was in the kitchen boiling up a stinking cow's head for the Rottweilers.

Ronnie was not in a good mood.

'I was listening to the radio today, and they said your boss had done a bunk. We'll never get the money for the bleedin' car now!'

'Yes we will!' Doreen slammed the fish and chips down on the table. 'Because I'm going to Spain to get it, that's why! I'm goin' on that 'oliday we never 'ad!' She took five plates out of the cupboard and started to share out the spoils.

'Spain? *Spain?* You can't go to bleedin' Spain?'

'Why not?' demanded Doreen, putting the ketchup and the HP sauce on the table.

'I'll tell you why not! Because we can't a-bleedin-fford it, that's why not!'

Ronnie was so overcome with indignation that he didn't even notice that he had put ketchup on the cow's head and handed his piece of haddock to Tiny.

'I can afford it, because I'm not payin'. Sandra fiddled the Petty Cash at work, put in a false invoice. She says if old man Fender's at it, she doesn't see why we shouldn't do it. We're all going, the Girls an' me.'

'What – now?'

'We're flyin' to Malaga tonight' said Doreen in triumph, and went upstairs to pack her crochet tops and her best white summer slacks.

'I think it's high time we all pooled our resources, don't you?'

Heidi looked first at Leofred, who was sitting on top of a suitcase tagged with a Sunstar Holidays label, and then at Jay Cathcart, who was lying on the bed with his Ray-Bans over his eyes, recovering from a lunchtime hangover. She had asked the two of them over to her new bedsit in Bayswater after Leofred had announced his imminent departure for Spain, on the trail of Clive Fender.

Jay was there because he was 'dating' Hilary Ardent, and Hilary worked for Boeler Sute Merchant Bank. In fact Jay was finding that he liked Hilary less and less. He usually went out with girls who were content to smile and say nothing and let him talk about himself, but Hilary only wanted to boast about how clever she was and how she was going to be the first woman director of Boeler Sute.

Leofred looked around the room at Heidi's new home. There were Grateful Dead posters covering the peeling paper on the walls, a tuber growing out of the sink and her smart new briefcase was doubling up as a coffee table. Yet he couldn't help noticing how well and happy Heidi seemed, sitting crossed legged on the floor in her night shirt, drinking beer out of a can. She was positively blooming, like a plant returned to its natural environment after a long spell in hot-house conditions.

'So . . .' she was saying, 'Jay, are you going to tell us what you found out today?'

Jay groaned.

'Jay had lunch with Hilary Ardent today,' Heidi explained. 'Jay? . . .'

'Three hours,' said Jay without opening his eyes. 'Three hours and God knows how much champagne . . . anyhow, she keeps talking about this guy she works for, Oliver Piddle . . . Riddle . . . something like that . . . she can't stand the guy for some reason, and says she's going to find a way to bring him down. Apparently Widdle reckons he's a bit of a big-shot and from the way he throws his money around he must be raking in more than his official salary.'

'Is that all?'

'Hey, give me a break,' groaned Jay. 'You've no idea what it's like trying to get the little vixen to talk about anything but herself. I really had to work out there! I've suffered grievous harm to the credit card.'

Jay lay back and pulled his Ray-Bans over his eyes again.

'Okay,' said Heidi. 'So what we have here is a set of coincidences, nothing more. There's a hard-fought take-over battle going on, and suddenly this Mr X is on the scene, moving shares around secretly. Meanwhile the chairman of Drummond appears to be giving company assets away in bribes, then runs off to Spain before the boys from the DTI come around. And Oliver Fiddle is apparently the man to watch at Boeler Sute, and he's the one whose initials are underlined in Fender's address book . . . But it's still coincidence. We need facts. Jay, are you willing to keep working on Hilary Ardent?'

Jay groaned again.

'Good. If we could only expose the identity of Mr X, then I'm sure everything else would fall into place. I suppose if the worst came to the worst, I could try the Janus's again . . .'

Heidi had drawn a veil over the reasons for her near miss in Kent.

' . . . so that leaves you, Leofred, and the biggest manhunt since the Great Train Robbery. I can just see the headlines now: "TYPING POOL BEAUTIES IN SPANISH STAKE-OUT" . . .'

'How about "PLUNKET 007"?' volunteered Jay, who had woken up again.

With as much dignity as he could muster, Leofred stood up and girded himself with his suitcase. 'I'd better get off to Gatwick now, or I'll miss the plane.'

'Well, good luck . . .' said Heidi, giving her brother a kiss on the cheek. 'Before you go, though, there's one thing I've been meaning to ask you . . . what exactly are you going to do with Fender when you find him?'

'What exactly are we going to do with him when we find him?' Leofred asked Sandra as they sat on the velour and chrome seats in the Gatwick Satellite. 'I mean, shouldn't we haave some sort of plan?'

'Listen everyone,' said Sandra loudly, putting her arm round Leofred's neck and rattling her ice-cubes in his ear. The others leaned forward in their seats. 'As far as I'm concerned, the reason we're going after Fender is to find out what he's done with Doreen's car. I mean, that's why we goot into all this, isn't it? All we want is for him to tell us where it is, or to give us the money. I don't really give a monkey's about anything else he's done. I reckon there's going to be plenty of other people worrying about that for us, eh, girls?'

The Girls chorused their agreement. An hour at the airport and they were all in high spirits. They had charged through passport control, clutching straw hats and inflatable lilos, with a great cry of 'Right! Let's get the drinks in! . . . Port and lemon for you, Doreen? . . .'

'Well, what else are you supposed to do at the beginning

of your holidays?' Sandra had said when she saw Leofred's horrified expression.

'But we're not even there yet.'

'Exactly. All the more reason to get pissed. Deadens the pain.'

Leofred sank back in his seat and surrendered to the inevitable. Doreen was on her third port and lemon and had started to sing the chorus of 'Una Paloma Blanca', which were the only words she knew. Out of the corner of one eye, Leofred could see a group of over-excited Club 18–30 passengers, who were playing a game that involved pouring the contents of lager cans over one another's heads and then using the empty cans as stilts.

The flight to Malaga was eventually called and passed in a blur of duty frees. The 18–30s threw bread rolls around the cabin and sang 'Oh, we're all off to sunny Spain . . . e VIVA Espana! . . .' Doreen who had never flown before, vomited into an in-flight sockette, mistaking it for a sick-bag.

At Malaga airport the Spanish ground staff looked on impassively as yet another rabble of drunken British tourists disembarked. The 18–30s snaked their way through immigration in a conga, and Leofred followed behind carrying Debbie's vanity case, Doreen's knitting and Sandra's beach bag.

Holiday reps. with coloured blazers and clipboards were directing people to awaiting coaches.

'Can anyone see our rep?' asked Carol. 'Look, that must be him – they said it'd be a local one.'

She pointed to a man holding up a sign with 'SUNSTAR HOLIDAES' written by hand. He was young and slim-hipped and had a Zapata moustache.

'Corr, get a load of that, eh?' hissed Sandra.

The Spaniard approached, grinning at the Girls. 'Hello,

my name eMiguel. I take you to Fuengirola. I hope you like?'

Sandra giggled. 'I'll tell you what *I'd* like, darlin' . . .' She blew him a kiss. Miguel responded by licking his lips. Sandra came back with a wiggle of the hips . . .

Leofred groaned and closed his eyes, not quite able to believe that he was standing in an airport lounge at three in the morning while two people overcame the international language barrier.

''Ere, leave it out Sandra!' complained Debbie. 'That's going it a bit, isn't it?'

Miguel picked up the heaviest suitcases. 'Plees, to come with me . . .'

'Aaaah! Innee sweet!' cooed Sandra. 'And the rest of you can lay off, he's mine . . .'

She set off after Miguel's swaying hips, singing 'We're all going to get laid . . . e viva espana! . . .'

Their minibus took them along the coast road, past the hills where the more wealthy holiday makers built their villas, and into the centre of the resort of Fuengirola. They rattled along the seafront and came to a halt outside a half-finished block of concrete.

'This Hotel Almeria,' said Miguel. 'This hotel belong my cousin. This hotel very nice—'

His speech was interrupted by the loud honking of a horn as a coach screeched up beside them and the 18–30s poured out of it and into the hotel.

'Many English people,' said Miguel, grinning. 'Very nice.'

The Almeria had no carpets and there was an empty hole where the lift shaft should have been, but at least it looked out over the sea and not the municipal dump, like some of the hotels they had passed. Each room had its own tiny balcony, adjacent to its neighbour, thus providing the

18–30s with a very convenient means of penetrating one another's rooms.

They wasted no time, and by the time Leofred started to unpack, the game of musical balconies had already begun. Through the thin walls he could hear Sandra next door, crashing the coat hangers in and out of the cardboard wardrobe.

''Ere Leof, look at this lot then!'

Sandra went out onto her balcony and Leofred joined her on his, a mere ten inches away. Below them was the beach ringed with an arc of concrete and coloured neon. The throb of disco music shook the hotel's foundations.

'Four o'clock in the morning and the joint's still jumping!' sighed Sandra. 'That's what I like to see!'

'I'll take you down there if you like,' offered Leofred, who had resigned himself to getting no sleep at all. 'We could take a look at some of the bars, see what's happening.'

Sandra reached across the balcony wall and patted his cheek. 'That's nice of you sweetheart, but no thanks. I slipped young Miguel my room number along with his tip, so it looks like old Auntie Sandra might get lucky tonight . . .' She giggled like a girl.

' . . . tell you what, though . . .' Before she went inside, she turned and looked out to the hills in the distance, and Leofred knew they were both thinking the same thing.

' . . . he's out there somewhere. And we're going to find him.'

Heidi Plunkett was doing her housework.

She swept all her clothes into a pile at the centre of the floor, scooped them up and pushed them under the bed. Then she seized the ancient carpet sweeper and ran it over the coffee stains and cigarette burns. It caught on the frayed edges of a hole and regurgitated all the dust and crumbs that it had scooped up in the past two years into a small mountain at the centre of the room.

'Shit!'

Heidi had just crouched down on all fours and was using her hands to sweep the dirt onto a back issue of the *Daily Meteor*, when the doorbell rang.

It was Ivo.

'Oh.' Heidi gripped the handle of the carpet sweeper like a machine gun.

He peered past her with a wistful expression. 'Can I come in?'

'Well, it's rather inconvenient actually, I'm expecting someone . . .

Ivo walked past her and stood at the centre of the room, with one polished shoe in the heap of carpet sweepings. He looked at the row of dirty coffee cups on the windowsill, at the overstuffed wardrobe with skirts hanging out of it and a door that refused to close, and his eyes lit up.

'This is a bit like your old place in Queen's Park, isn't it?'

'Yes, it is, now if you—'

'The reason I came over was to bring you this.' Studiously ignoring Heidi's impatience, Ivo reached into his jacket pocket and pulled out some letters. 'The mail that came to the flat.'

Heidi sniffed. 'Why didn't you get one of your minions to bring it over. I would have thought you'd be far too busy to think of such trivialities when you're in the middle of a takeover bid.'

'Well, as you know, next week's the closing week, so it's just a matter of tidying up the details—'

'And how convenient for you that the opposition's been knocked out by a scandal,' said Heidi sourly.

Ivo shrugged. 'I wouldn't say that. Drummond stock has

fallen slightly since the start of the week, but it's still high. It's only rumour so far, they haven't got any evidence . . . which reminds me, how's your article coming on?'

Heidi didn't reply.

'Well, if there's anything I can help you with,' Ivo walked towards the door and paused with his hand on the doorknob, 'anything I can tell you . . . You only have to ask me.'

Heidi let out a howl of rage and flung the carpet sweeper after Ivo's retreating figure. It hit the door and exploded, sending a second volley of crumbs and dirt around the room.

She had just finished attending to the damage when the doorbell rang again. Thanks to Ivo's visit, there had been no time to get ready, and instead of the alluring figure she had hoped to present, she was dirty and dishevelled. She grabbed a bottle of wine and two glasses and arranged them on top of a stereo speaker. There was just time to dab a bottle of scent against her neck, but she tipped it up too far, and about a quarter of a pint of it ran down her shoulder and drenched her T-shirt.

Reeking of Opium, she flung open the door and found a six-foot bouquet of hot-house blooms, with Conrad Janus's face just visible amongst the foliage.

He placed the flowers in her arms and she staggered backwards. 'How lovely . . . Come in.'

The bouquet was so enormous that it was as if the room had been taken over by a forest. There was no space on the floor big enough to take them, and if she laid them down on the bed, then one of them would be left with nowhere to sit. Heidi tried sticking them behind the radiator, but they obscured the window and plunged the room into total darkness. She propped them against the wardrobe door, but they toppled over, knocking the wine and glasses off the speaker.

'If you'll excuse me, I'll just go and put these in water . . .'

Looking like a moving tree, she carried the flowers to the communal bathroom and dumped them in the bath. When she came back into her room, she was knocked backwards by the smell of the spilt perfume. Conrad was standing in the middle of the room with his hands in his pockets and the air of a man waiting for a flight to be called. He looked so devastatingly handsome with his Mediterranean tan and his crisp, dark curls, that once again Heidi felt desire go straight from eye to groin, bypassing the brain, and she wanted to fling herself on the bed in a seductive pose.

But she remembered her failure the last time, and knew that she couldn't afford two such mistakes.

'The reason I asked you over here,' she began, ' . . . Was to get the number of that useful go-between you mentioned. I've got a large sum of money to invest, and . . .'

Her voice tailed off as she saw the look on Conrad's face.

He looked around the room, and then at her, and she could see the growing suspicion in his eyes. He was wondering why she lived in a squalid bedsit if she had so much money, and he was probably also wondering how on earth she had managed to be invited to his house in Kent with someone who obviously wasn't her boyfriend . . . he had probably even noticed the large pile of press cuttings on the floor and started to put two and two together.

I should never have invited him here, she thought. If only I was still living in the apartment in St Katherine's Dock . . .

Conrad was still waiting for her to explain herself, and she realised that she had no choice but to distract him. She arranged herself on the bed in the seductive pose that she had earlier vetoed.

' . . . But we can talk business later.' She gave him a

smile that would have put Lorelei to shame. 'Why don't you come over here and get comfortable?'

'Here? You can't be serious!'

Heidi looked at him, uncomprehending.

'Look at it – it's a bid sordid, isn't it? . . . I'll tell you what, why don't we go back to my hotel?'

Heidi acquiesced, though by now she was feeling confused about her motives, climbing into Conrad's Lamborghini without a murmur and allowing him to drive her to the Dorchester.

As soon as they were in his suite with the door closed, Conrad started to undress.

'I'm just going to have a quick shower. Be a good girl and jump into bed . . .' He glanced at his watch. ' . . . I've got forty minutes.'

Heidi sat down on the edge of the emperor size bed, but she did not undress. Instead she picked up Conrad's jacket and started going through the pockets. As she had suspected, he kept an Organofax (gold-tooled Morocco) bulging with information. She started to flick through the pages.

Predictably, there were no names listed under 'X'. Undeterred, Heidi turned to the 'Notes' section and ran a cursory eye over each page until she found what she was looking for. Pencilled across one corner of a page was an equation: 'X = 794 3235.' She copied the number onto the inside of her wrist and pulled her sleeve over it.

The sound of gushing water was still audible from the bathroom, but she was sure that if Conrad said a quick shower, he meant a quick shower. She stared at the morocco organofax and overpowering nosiness won over caution. She opened the diary section.

Her own name was written in with '6pm' beside it. Underneath that was 'Lorna – 8pm'. So Conrad really was going to call time after forty minutes. He was a busy man.

Throughout the week there were similar entries under the headings 'Sara', 'Kerry', and 'Annabel'.

Before replacing the Organofax in his jacket, Heidi took one last look in the leather pouch at the back. Three packets of black condoms fell out, and a florist's bill. It was for six identical hot-house bouquets – deluxe size.

There was now the buzzing of an electric shaver in the bathroom. No doubt Conrad was trying to save time before the next appointment. Heidi stared at the closed bathroom door for a second while the last glimmer of temptation flickered and died, then crept quietly from the room.

It was only when she had left the Dorchester behind her and was standing in the street, that she realised what she had done. By disappearing like that, she would have confirmed all Conrad's suspicions about her. He would be in no doubt now that she was investigating his activities and would almost certainly have concluded that she was a journalist. Mr X would be tipped off, and worse still he might try to sabotage her enquiries . . . he might even send someone after her to stop her by force . . .

Fear had made her break involuntarily into a run, and she headed down Park Lane at top speed, glancing over her shoulder and scattering clusters of American tourists. She continued down the Bayswater Road, not stopping until she came to Cleveland Square and the safety of her bedsit.

By the time she had run up the steps and unlocked the front door – stopping only to check that no-one was following her – she was too busy trying to get her breath back to notice the long white car waiting in the shadows for her safe return.

In the head offices of Boeler Sute merchant Bank, a deadly

hush had fallen. It was Friday, and in the City of London, Friday was POETS day – Piss Off Early, Tomorrow's Saturday. The cleaners had finished dusting the marble-topped tables in the reception area, and had arranged the glossy magazines in neat piles. The front doors were locked. The only sound was the low hum of the air-conditioning . . .

. . . And a high-pitched giggling.

Inside the glass-screened security booth, out of sight, Hilary Ardent was sitting on Steve Dibney's lap, surrounded by the flickering monitor screens.

Hilary unbuttoned Steve's shirt to reveal his hairy rug of a chest, then removed his security guard's peaked cap and placed it on her smooth golden head. He lunged for her.

'Like women in uniform do you' . . . she whispered. ' . . . Hey, wait a minute, what's that?' She pushed Steve's hand away from her stocking top and pointed at the screen that monitored the twelfth floor.

'Fucking hell there's someone in the building . . .' He stood up and peered closer. 'It's okay, it's only that pratt Riddle.'

'Probably working late.'

'More likely hanging around waiting for you . . .'

'Well, he's obviously waiting for someone – look.'

Riddle was standing in the area near the lift, checking his watch anxiously. Then, as Hilary and Steve watched, the lift doors slid open and a man stepped out. He was slightly built, wearing dark glasses and carrying a small suitcase.

'How the fuck did he get in?' said Steve. 'The front doors were locked hours ago . . . he must have sneaked in through the goods entrance . . .' There was a certain amount of grudging admiration in his voice.

He lost interest in Riddle's affairs and tried to envelop

Hilary in a lecherous embrace, but she pushed him aside, still staring up at the screen.

'Quick!' she said, and pointed at the panel of buttons on the monitor console. 'How do you get this machine to record? I want to get a picture of this!'

Up on the television screen, Riddle gave a quick glance around him, then handed the man a briefcase.

'Well go on, you great lump!' screamed Hilary. 'Quickly!'

Steve stared at the flickering image for a split second, then lunged forward and pressed the 'Video Record' button, just as the man lifted the lid of the briefcase and revealed the contents.

'Well fuck me – it's full of cash!'

In the sweltering heat of Fuengirola, even Leofred's headache had a disco beat.

He was walking along the esplanade with Sandra in search of refreshment. Most of her face was obscured by her floppy-brimmed hat, dark glasses and Factor 15 sunblock, but the bits that were visible were scowling. Young Miguel's passion had started to cool, and she was in a foul temper.

They sat down outside an establishment called the Liverpool Bar, which boasted 'Taylor's Yorkshire Tea.'

'Just elike your Mamma she emake!' said the sycophantic waiter as he put the insipid liquid down in front of them.

Sandra peered into the cup. 'My mum would rather have cut her own throat than serve tea like that,' she observed.

Leofred knew that anything he said would worsen Sandra's mood, so he preserved a tactful silence and devoted himself to surveying the colourful local scene. Next door at the Wonky Donkey Disco, which screened twenty-four hour rock videos, an irate British holidaymaker, accompanied by a bilious looking friend, was complaining to the management.

'But I know I left my shades here last night!' he shouted in a thick Birmingham accent. 'Because this was the last place I saw them!'

The manager gesticulated and shouted back in Spanish. The holidaymaker thumped him in the mouth. His companion threw up into a beer barrel converted into an ashtray.

They had left the other Girls on the beach. Debbie and Carol were stretched out on the grey, gritty sand. Every so often they would ask one another 'Am I brown yet?' and yank down the side of their bikini bottoms to compare marks. Doreen was sitting next to them reading an article in 'Woman's Treasure' about how to crochet one of Princess Margaret's hats.

Leofred stared into the middle distance, and caught sight of a group of 18–30s, waiting on a jetty to board their Pirate Cruise. This outing involved their usual activities of stripping off their clothes and getting disgustingly drunk, but they were carried out on board a boat that terrorised the coastline, sailing into unspoilt bays and spoiling them.

Sandra slammed her cup down into her saucer. 'Bloody hell, it's *him!*' she yelled. 'There – just coming out of that greengrocer's!'

Leofred looked up and saw Clive Fender wearing a false beard and holding a large cucumber.

'Well come on, don't just sit there – after him!'

Sandra was galvanised into action. She flung a handful of pesetas in the direction of the confused waiter and hurried down the street on the trail of her prey, with Leofred scurrying along behind.

Fender headed towards the main shopping street at the centre of the town, and disappeared into an establishment called Sergio's English Supermarket. Sandra and Leofred hung back in the doorway and watched him through the shop window.

Fender was wearing a red T-shirt, that conspired with the false beard to make him look like a displaced Santa Claus. Beneath his shorts, his legs were white like raw chicken flesh.

'Hasn't got a very good tan, has he?' observed Sandra disparagingly.

He was wandering about in the supermarket, staring at things on the shelves as though he wasn't really seeing them. In the end he picked up a jar of Marmite and a bottle of Worcestershire sauce and carried them to the checkout desk.

While he paid for them, Sandra and Leofred flattened themselves against the wall, Starsky and Hutch style. Then the chase was on again.

Fender turned off the main shopping street and through a series of narrow alleys until he came to the unsurfaced track that led to the hills. He started to walk up it, leaving the town behind him. Sandra and Leofred followed at a remove of fifty yards, until he hailed a passing taxi cab and jumped into it.

'We'll never keep up with him now!' moaned Leofred as the taxi disappeared in a cloud of dust.

But Sandra was more resourceful. A cart came trundling up the road behind them, pulled by a donkey and driven by a wizened Spanish peasant.

'Oi, mush! Give us a ride, eh, there's a love!'

The driver bared blackened teeth and muttered something quite incomprehensible.

'That's all right, darlin', we don't mind if it's not very comfy . . . come on, budge up!'

Sandra squeezed on to the seat next to the driver. 'Follow that cab!' she yelled. 'Ooh . . . I've always wanted to say that!' With Leofred rolling around in the back with the smelly cargo of rotting vegetables and greasy clothing, they bounced their way up the hill. The taxi was still out of sight.

Quite unconcerned by his lack of English, Sandra chattered away to the driver until they were firm friends and he was grinning and nodding enthusiastically.

' . . . Fuengirola's a nice little place isn't it? . . . only I don't suppose you get much chance to go out to the discos do you? . . . I don't suppose your missus'll let you . . . so what's this stick for then? . . . what happens if I jus' give Neddy a bit of a tap on the bum with it? . . .'

Sandra picked up the driver's whip and slapped the donkey's backside with it until the poor beast was practically galloping up the hill, with the cart rattling violently and Leofred offering up silent prayers as he gripped its sides.

'Ooh look, we've caught up with them!'

They were now in sight of the taxi again. It had pulled up outside a concealed entrance, and Fender was paying off the driver.

Sandra jumped down from the cart. ''ere Leof, pass us my bag, quick!'

She groped around until she found her instamatic camera, and took a snap of Fender, shopping bag in hand, unlocking a pair of heavy wrought iron gates.

'Evidence,' she explained.

Taking care to stay out of sight, they followed Fender up a long driveway to a low white villa with terracotta roof tiles. Sprinklers were playing over springy green lawns, and a burly Spanish gardener was chopping the dead heads off the roses.

He eyed the intruders with hostility.

'Buenos dias!' trilled Sandra. *'Did you see that? Talk about hunky . . .'*

126

'Surely we're not just going to ring the doorbell?' Leofred asked when they reached the front porch.

'Why not?' Sandra challenged.

Leofred did. The door was opened by Mrs Marjorie Fender, a well-preserved forty-ish with a dark tan and a peach-coloured play suit. Her face wore the sort of smile that tells you she's not really pleased to see you.

'We'd like to speak to Mr Clive Fender, please.'

'I'm sorry, he's not here,' said Marjorie Fender, closing the door.

Quick as a flash, Sandra jammed it open with a five inch white patent stiletto. 'Wait a minute – we've just seen him.'

'You must be mistaken. My husband is away on business.'

'A likely story!' scoffed Sandra as the door slammed in their faces. 'Oh well, we'll just have to come back after it's dark.'

'Why after it's dark?' Leofred wanted to know.

'Because that's what they always do on telly. Anyway, it'll be something to do, won't it? I'm bored with discos . . .'

It was Friday night, and Friday night was limbo night at the Almeria Hotel.

A space had been cleared in the dining room, and grown-up men who in real life were electricians, civil servants and carpet salesmen had put on grass skirts and paper flowers and were wriggling under a broom handle held twelve inches off the ground. They clapped in time to the music to cheer their friends' efforts, and shouted hysterically like five-year-olds at a birthday party. If there had been ice cream and jelly, they would have thrown it.

' . . . And remember!' the English rep. in frilly dress shirt boomed, his lips too near to the microphone. 'The contest is not just for the guys . . . Any of you lovely ladies want to have a go?'

There was much nudging and egging on. Finally, after cries of '*Go on!*' from Debbie, Carol and Jenny, Doreen Thwort raised her hand and someone hurried off to fetch her a grass skirt.

Doreen blushed and giggled but soon her inhibitions were lost in the bravado of the moment and she was thrusting her plump hips under the broomhandle with a steely determination.

'Come on Doe!' shrieked the Girls, taking the role of official cheerleaders, and the other onlookers clapped her to an outright victory.

'Bleedin' 'ell – me arthritis!' said a flushed Doreen, just as the compère thrust the microphone in front of her mouth.

He quickly snatched it back again. 'And that was Mrs Doreen Thwort from London, ladies and gents, give her a big hand, please . . .'

There was a round of drunken applause and the grass-skirted lads lifted Doreen onto their shoulders for a lap of honour.

' . . . And now our disco is about to begin, ladies and gents, kicking off with Black Lace and "Agadoo" . . .'

Leofred and Sandra sat on high stools at the bar, drinking cocktails with a lot of plastic flowers stuffed into them. Sandra was watching the faithless Miguel dancing with Debbie, rolling his eyes and thrusting his snakey hips. She was pretending not to notice, but there was venom in her eyes.

'Disgusting . . .' she muttered to herself, clutching her handbag like a grenade.

Now Miguel had pulled Debbie into his arms and was undulating his pelvis around the floor to the strains of Julio Inglesias.

'Let's go, sunshine,' said Sandra abruptly, pushing her

drink away from her and climbing down from her stool. She grabbed Leofred by the cuff of his jacket and used her not inconsiderable strength to pull him out into the street. There was a tacit agreement that only the two of them should go to Fender's villa that night, so without further discussion Leofred hailed a cab and asked the driver to take them up into the hills.

There was no street lighting of any sort, and no other houses nearby, so when they climbed out of the cab it was into total blackness.

'Bloody hell, it's dark!' complained Sandra, who was starting to get the giggles.

They groped their way towards the iron gates and found them locked. Leofred, who was being eaten alive by mosquitos, was ready to give up and go home, but he already knew that Sandra wouldn't sanction such a move.

'We'll have to climb over it.'

'What – dressed like that?'

'Cybill Shepherd does it in *Moonlighting*,' replied Sandra as though an American TV show could justify by example clambering up a twenty foot iron gate dressed in spike heels and flowered silk rayon with plunging front and wrap-over skirt. She proceeded to prove that it could be done, ripping the hem of her skirt and swearing loudly.

Leofred climbed onto the gate to begin his ascent and was rewarded by coarse giggling from somewhere at the top of the gate. 'Good job it's so bleedin' dark, or you'd be looking right up my bum . . .'

'*Shit!* . . .'

Safely on firm ground on the other side, Leofred tripped over a garden sprinkler and stubbed his toe.

'Shhhh! They've probably got a dog . . . and I'm not talking about his wife,' said Sandra, who had taken a dislike to Marjorie Fender on their earlier meeting.

They tiptoed up to the house and climbed in through a

ground floor window, after first sliding back the mosquito screen. Sandra slithered through first and landed upside down on the carpet with her skirt over her head.

'You were right,' she whispered, 'I should have worn trousers . . .' Pulling herself into a sitting position, and smoothing her hair, she went on, 'Right – next we've got to try and work out which is Fender's bedroom..'

Leofred's more cautious nature came into play, and he tried to imagine a scenario in which he and Sandra burst in on the sleeping couple and demanded justice. It was impossible.

'What are we going to say when we find him?'

'Well . . . we're going to confront him, aren't we?'

'But he'll be asleep—'

'Not for long! . . .'

They identified the master bedroom from the humming of a lone air conditioner, and stood poised outside the door.

Sandra straightened her skirt. 'Ready?'

Leofred nodded.

The door was flung open with a reverberating crash.

In the dim light, it was just possible to discern the outline of a hump-backed shape at the centre of the double bed. The light from the window cast its shadow on the wall, moving to and fro in dumb-show.

'Blimey!' whispered Sandra, 'I wouldn't have thought old Bender still had it in him! . . . oh well, here goes! . . .'

She flicked on the light switch.

The two halves of the lump separated and Marjorie Fender peered out indignantly from beneath the sheet. So did her muscular Spanish gardener.

Leofred and Sandra retreated into the darkness of the landing, stifling laughter and waiting for pursuit.

'We'd better leave now,' whispered Leofred, who calculated that they had about as long as it took for a Spaniard to put on his trousers.

'Aw . . . I'm just beginning to enjoy meself..let's just check a couple of the other bedrooms . . . oh, shit there's a ghost, look!'

'Who's there?' demanded the sepulchral figure, switching on a lamp. It was Clive Fender wearing white silk pyjamas and brandishing a hand-gun. He said nothing, but waved the gun in the direction of Leofred's crotch.

'It's us,' said Leofred rather feebly. 'Ah . . . from Drummond. You remember Sandra, from Typing, I'm sure, and my name's Leofred Plunkett. Your new graduate recruit.'

Fender – who obviously didn't remember either of them – automatically reached out to shake hands as if they were at an office Christmas party, but the gun got in the way.

'I can't think why you're out here' he said crossly. 'Didn't Marjorie hear the doorbell?'

'We came through the window.'

'In that case, you're breaking and entering! Go on – shoo!' Fender waved the gun again.

'Perhaps we could go through into your lounge,' suggested Sandra helpfully. 'We're here on company business.'

'I can't discuss business now – I'm on holiday. And you're trespassing—'

'It's about the matter of Doreen's car,' said Sandra, going into the sitting room anyway.

'Doreen?' Fender shambled after her, his pyjama trousers gaping. He didn't have his glasses on and couldn't see very well without them.

'You remember Doreen . . .' Sandra picked up a marble ashtray in the shape of a sombrero and examined it carefully. 'Your tea-lady. She won the Daimler in the prize draw. You remember the Daimler, I take it . . .'

'Ah yes,' Fender had woken up at last, and was growing nervous. His forehead was sweating. 'The car . . . I've been meaning to sort out the problem. Been meaning to send Mrs Thwort a cheque, actually . . . Drink, anyone?'

Fender now had the gun in one hand and a decanter of scotch in the other.

'We'll have it now.'

'A scotch?—'

'The cheque.'

Sandra stood over Fender while he wrote a cheque for twenty-five-thousand pounds with a trembling hand. She stuffed it into her bra, then nodded Leofred in the direction of the door.

'Wait a minute,' said Leofred. 'I've got a few questions for Mr Fender myself . . . like why did he empty the company safe before he came here? . . .'

Fender had turned very pale, and was trembling violently.

' . . . why he failed to keep his appointment with the Department of Trade and Industry inspectors? . . .'

He was crumbling now, right in front of their eyes.

' . . . and whether he's made the acquaintance of an underground arbitrageur known as "Mr X".'

'*You!*' hissed Fender furiously, 'You're a reporter aren't you? You've been spying on us all along . . . you're a bloody *mole!*'

He raised the barrel of the gun and fired it at Leofred.

Owing to his short sight he missed, and hit the sombrero lighter instead, sending fragments of marble riccocheting around the room.

'Come on Hercule Poirot,' said Sandra. She grabbed the thunderstruck Leofred by the scruff of the neck at the precise moment the sitting room doors opened to admit a hysterical Marjorie Fender and her semi-naked lover.

'Time we left this lot to it . . .'

Seven

Heidi Plunkett picked up her new cordless telephone and punched in the number.

She repeated it out loud as she did so, to be absolutely sure that she was dialling the right one.

'Seven – nine – four, three – two – three – five . . .'

Three rings, a click and a bleep.

'You have just reached 794 3235. Thank you for calling. Please leave your name and number after the tone and your call will be returned as soon as possible. Beeeeep—'

Heidi sighed and hung up. There wasn't any point in leaving her name again. She had already left three messages. She searched under the bed for her shoes, swept the papers and toast crumbs off her briefcase and set off for work.

Driving to Fleet Street, she was overcome with frustration and a sense of failure. The closing date for the Star takeover bids was looming, and she had no material for her article, other than the speculative scenario that she and Jay and Leofred had dredged together. She could guess at enough to write a brilliant exposé, but she couldn't make it stand up. Any editor would therefore reject it.

Heidi was still convinced that Mr X was the key to

the whole operation, but had abandoned any hope of ever exposing him. Stealing his phone number from Conrad Janus had seemed both a stroke of daring and a brilliant piece of journalism, but she had been too busy congratulating herself to consider the possibility that the phone number would be useless. She had even pulled strings to jump the British Telecom waiting list and have her own line installed in her bedsit. But no-one ever answered at the house in Bishop's Avenue, apart from the answering machine. She left her name and number, but of course Mr X did not telephone her. He relied on introductions. Personal contact.

She was so absorbed in maudlin reflection that she failed to notice a parked delivery van in Holborn, and scraped several inches of immaculate paint from her Mercedes. By the time she stomped into the *Meteor* building, she was in a thoroughly bad mood.

In the newsroom, reporters were standing at their desks bellowing abuse down the phones, screwing up their copy and throwing it onto the floor, threatening to kill one another, themselves, or the editor – though not necessarily in that order. In other words it was a normal day. Heidi walked past oblivious, into the lesser uproar of the features department and saw exactly what she had been dreading seeing. A message on her desk that read: '*9 a.m. Ross Hopper would like to see you as soon as you get in.*'

Ross Hopper was not a happy man. He had his bottle of Glenlivet on the desk, and this time he made no attempt to hide it, not even at ten in the morning.

'We're losing it,' he said as Heidi walked in. He shook his head slowly and gulped at the scotch, repeating 'We're losing it, you know, losing it.'

'Losing it?' enquired Heidi, wondering if the *Meteor*, too, was to be the subject of a takeover.

'Our exclusive.' He stabbed a finger in the direction of

his desk, which was spread with rival daily papers. 'That's the trouble, you see, Heidi, if you leave it too long before jumping in, someone else gets in there first . . .'

Heidi submitted to the ensuing string of journalistic clichés without comment. She did not remind Hopper that in the course of duty she had split up with her lover, involved herself in a bizarre bondage session and risked being bombed by Armenian terrorists. Or the fact that she had put her brother's job at risk and induced one of her best friends to act as a mole. Instead she took the two clippings that Hopper was holding out to her, and read them in silence.

'TRANSATLANTIC TWIST TO STAR TAKE-OVER?' wondered the first. 'Yesterday the City was reeling at the rumours of a last minute bid to buy the Star Group. US industrialist, Hyman Weevil (pictured above) would make no comment about his alleged eleventh hour attempt to oust competitors Rapier and the troubled Drummond Industries. Weevil, 59, originally founded his fortune on incontinence pads, but has recently made a spectacular departure into baby wipes. He declined to discuss the seeming impossibility of raising share support at this late stage in the proceedings, but it is known that last night he flew from his native Kentucky to New York for discussions with financial advisors . . .'

Heidi looked at the picture of Hyman Weevil. He was wearing a ten, possibly fifteen, gallon hat and a spectacular pair of dentures. His cheeks were polished and rosy like apples.

'The bastard!' said Hopper with feeling, pouring whisky directly from the bottle to his gullet. 'I mean this really screws it up now, doesn't it? America, for Christ's sake! This thing is getting out of hand . . . What does that red-necked bastard think he's playing at? We'll never be able to keep tabs on *him* as well as all the other crooks, not if we're talking the other side of the Atlantic . . .'

Heidi did not attempt to interrupt this rant. Instead she took the other article from his frantically waving hand and read it.

'*The Square Mile thrives on gossip and no-one is more gossipped about lately than mysterious master arbitrageur, "Mr X". Stories centre not so much on how he does it as who he is. The most popular theory is that he is an ex-merchant banker with a grudge against the financial establishment at large and his former employers in particular. After keeping what is generally presumed to be his home under close surveillance, our reporter can confirm that Mr X is no longer in this country. Possibly he fears the effects of ever-growing media attention . . . '*

This article also had a picture to illustrate it. The house in Bishop's Avenue, complete with drawn curtains, security gates and stone griffins.

'Shit!' said Heidi. She helped herself to a mouthful of Hopper's scotch.

'You see what I mean? I've got to have that article, Heidi, and I've got to have it fast.'

'But—'

'I want it on my desk by Friday. You've got four days.'

At Gatwick Airport, a charter flight from Malaga had just landed and was regurgitating its passengers onto the runway.

Clad in skimpy shorts and vests to flaunt their glowing tans to the weary, pasty-faced airport staff, they charged down the steps clutching donkeys and Spanish costume dolls and clanking bags of duty frees.

Leofred was swept along by the crowd, in the direction of Baggage Reclaim, wondering why he was the only person who seemed to be exhausted by their five a.m. departure time. He stood at the edge of the carousel and watched the same few suitcases go past again and again.

'You're peeling.' observed Sandra, raking a long, red nail over his blistered shoulder. Sheets of skin fell away. She looked admiringly at her own chocolate coloured forearm, then held it next to Debbie's and noted with satisfaction that it was browner.

'You got a lovely colour there, Sand.' said Debbie humbly, still trying to placate Sandra after the theft of Miguel.

'Yes, well, I would have. People who spend all their time in bed when the sun's shining don't get so brown, do they? . . .'

Sandra ignored Debbie and turned back to Leofred. 'But we had a great time though, didn't we, eh?' She draped her arm heavily around Leofred's shoulder. 'You and I are mates, aren't we? . . . we're muckers, we are. We make a great team.'

They looked at Doreen, who was sipping a sticky pink liqueur from her duty free bag.

' . . . and we managed to do what we said we were going to do. We got her money back. I reckon the trip was a complete success.'

Leofred, thinking of Heidi and her expectations, was not so sure. He gave a despairing sigh.

'Oh, come on misery guts!' She pointed to Doreen, who had now put away her bottle and was practising the flamenco with a pair of plastic castanets. 'At least we've made *her* happy!'

Doreen Thwort was still humming a haunting hispanic air when she climbed out on to the pavement outside

32, Ingledew Road, Plumstead. She had taken the unprecedented step of arriving home in a taxi.

'*Bleedin' ell!*'. Ronnie came down the path in his slippers, with Tiny and Nipper completing the welcoming committee. 'A bleedin' taxi! What do you think we are, made of money?'

Doreen pushed past him, a knowing smile on her face.

Ronnie stared. 'What – you don't mean? . . . you mean you got the bleedin' money?'

Doreen nodded and went into the lounge. She sank down onto the sofa and put her feet up on the leatherette pouffe. 'Put the kettle on, will you love. I'm dying for a decent cup of tea! They couldn't make it for toffee in Spain. Not that there wasn't plenty of other things to drink, mind! Shall I tell you what they used to give us for breakfast. We used to have these funny little rolls, and then . . .'

Doreen launched into a long and tedious travelogue, while Ronnie and the dogs went into the kitchen.

'Never mind about the bleedin' poolside buffets!' he shouted, 'What about the money? How much you got? I want to make a start on that crazy paving . . .'

Doreen ignored him and babbled on. ' . . . The weather was ever so hot, you wouldn't believe how hot it was! Hundred in the shade, someone said . . . well, it wasn't quite so bad in the evenings; you used to have to put a cardi on sometimes . . . and they had these little fridges in all the bedrooms – well, mine didn't work, but I used to put my drinks in Carol's fridge . . . oh, and I must tell you, Ronnie, they had this limbo-dancing contest in the hotel one night, and you'll never guess who won it! . . . we was up till ever so late, most nights, I don't know how I kept going, I really don't, mind you when you've nothing to do but sit on a beach all day. There's going to be some really funny photos of all us lot, I can't wait to see them.

Sandra said she'd have us all over one night and we could have a Spanish evening and look at them all . . .'

Sammi-Dawn stomped down into the lounge, puffy-eyed and yawning. She was wearing baby-doll pyjamas and a pair of high-heeled slippers trimmed with pink marabou feathers. She clomped past her mother without seeing her and into the hall, where the household's one phone was located.

She dialled the number of Rapier's head office and was put through to Ivo's secretary.

'It's extremely personal and urgent.' she said in as haughty a tone as she could. 'It's his wife, in fact.'

Ivo came onto the line.

'Have you asked her yet?'

'*Sammi-Dawn, I've asked you not lie about who you are when you ring me. Now if you don't mind . . .*'

'I only want to know if you've asked her.'

'*Sammi, how many times do I have to tell you, I don't have the opportunity any more. We haven't seen one another since she moved out and I wouldn't have any influence with her if I did. If I were you, I'd forget about it and find something else to do with your time—*'

Sammi slammed the phone down. 'Well you can go and fuck yourself!' she muttered, and went back into the lounge.

'Sammi, I was just telling your Dad about Spain . . .' said Doreen. 'And look, I bought you this . . .' She reached into her bag and bought out a skimpy pink T-shirt printed with 'My mum went to Fuengirola and all she bought me was this lousy T-shirt', ' . . . you would have loved it there, Sam, you really would! You should have seen the discos! And all them dishy Spanish blokes. Did I tell you, Sandra had her eye on one, and then Debbie . . .'

Sammi had already clumped her way up the stairs again, T-shirt in hand.

Doreen raised an eyebrow. 'What's the matter with madam then? What did I say?'

Ronnie shrugged. 'She's had a real gob on her for days now. I reckon it's this.'

He handed Doreen a copy of the *Daily Meteor* 'Who will be our fabulous chick of the Year?' screamed the headline. 'Only four more days to go!'

Leofred returned from Gatwick to his bedsit in Maida Vale, only to be summoned straight out again to a crisis meeting by Heidi.

'It's really urgent Leof, I promise! I'm at Jay's studio in Wardour Street. Can you catch a cab and come straight over? . . .'

'Clive Fender tried to kill me,' he told the others as they sat amid the stripped pine floorboards and Swiss cheese plants at Rapier Promotions. He thought he may as well start on a positive note.

'Could you use an attempted murder charge as leverage over him?' asked Heidi hopefully.

'Well, he pointed the gun at my private parts . . .'

'That only makes him look as if he's crazy.'

'He is.' said Leofred gloomily.

Heidi sighed, and ran a hand through her hair, which was none too clean. There were shadows under her eyes and her face had a tense, drawn look. Having not smoked for years, she lit a cigarette. 'Did you at least get a picture?'

'I got this.' Leofred handed her the picture that Sandra had taken, showing Fender with false beard and shopping bag.

'It's a start, I suppose, but we still don't really have proof of anything. After all, you did break into his house. He could give that as a reason for turning a gun on you. What we need is something in writing linking him and Riddle and Mr X. Do you think there's anything lying around at Drummond?'

Leofred shook his head. 'The Girls went through everything in the computer. And Fender emptied the safe himself.'

He saw the look on his sister's face and went on. 'It's only an article, Heidi. And you've done your best with it. Just tell them that's all they're going to get.'

Heidi dragged on the cigarette and shook her head. 'I can't do that. It's not just that I'll be relegated to writing articles about Princess Diana's diet problems. I *know* there's something going on. For my own satisfaction I've got to tie the whole thing together.'

'But you've only got four days . . .'

'I know – it's hopeless.'

At that moment Jay switched his attention from the girl in a very tight black mini skirt bending over to water the cheeseplants, to the matter in hand.

'Hey, listen kid, you just leave it all to your uncle Jay.'

'Go boil your head, Jay!'

No, I'm serious. We could be talking wrap-up city here. We are dealing with hard evidence, and when I say *hard*, I mean hard, like—'

'Cut the crap Jay, and get to the point.'

'Hilary Ardent told me that she had got a photograph of Riddle handing some guy a cash bribe. Taken with a security camera at the bank.'

'Jay! Why on earth didn't you mention this before?'

Jay looked vague. 'I suppose I forgot.' He snapped his fingers at Black Mini-skirt and told her to bring him a mineral water. 'Anyone else want refreshment?'

'Never mind that! What about this picture? Can you get a copy?'

Jay sucked his teeth. 'Difficult. Very difficult . . .'

'Please, Jay!'

'Well, I guess I can try.'

'You'll have to – it's our last bloody chance.' Heidi extinguished her cigarette and stood up wearily. She gave Jay's shoulder a squeeze. 'I'm counting on you . . .'

Oliver Riddle was sitting at his desk at Boeler Sute, staring at the financial pages of the *Times*.

'*FOUR DAYS TO CLOSE OF STAR BID . . .*'

The telephone rang. Riddle took the call on his special debugged line.

'Hello? . . . No, I can't possibly fly over there myself . . . It's out of the question . . . far too risky—'

He suddenly became aware of someone standing in the doorway, watching him. He looked up into the foxy green eyes of Hilary Ardent.

She gave him a winsome smile and he breathed a little faster as he started to imagine reasons why she should have come to his office suddenly, unannounced . . .

'Sorry to interrupt, Mr Riddle, but I wanted to know if you'd mind me taking a long lunch break today?'

Riddle frowned. Ever since the picnic episode he had been hyper-sensitive on the subject of Hilary's social life.

' . . . Only I have to go and see my gynaecologist. You know, it's women's problems . . .' Hilary lowered her eyes and looked modestly at the floor, murmuring 'Ever since the incident in Dickens and Jones . . .

'Of course, of course.' Riddle turned red. 'Take as long as you need m'dear. Well go on then, run along!'

Run was exactly what Hilary did. She picked up her briefcase and hurried out of the building with a self-satisfied smirk on her face. She had twisted one man round her little finger and was about to do the same with a second. She was going to meet Jay Cathcart for lunch.

Jay had booked them a private room at Chez Victor and filled it with fresh flowers. He seemed unusually nervous, and Hilary decided to behave as if there was nothing at all out of the ordinary about these lavish favours. After giving the flowers a cursory glance, she sat down at the table and smoothed her napkin over her lap with one hand while holding up the menu for critical scrutiny with the other.

'Hey, I got you this.' Jay pushed a small velvet box across the tablecloth.

Hilary opened it and took out a gold chain with a diamond teardrop hanging from it.

'Pretty,' was all she said.

She was pretending that she didn't know why Jay was making such a fuss of her, when of course she knew exactly what he wanted.

'Ur . . . hey, listen,' he said after he had sent back a bottle of champagne because Hilary complained that it was not cold enough, 'Do you remember that photograph you were telling me about?'

'Mmmm' said Hilary, pretending to be more interested in running her pink, pointed little tongue around an oyster.

'Well do you think that, like . . . you might let me see it?'

Hilary smiled. How thrilling it was to have so much power! 'Well now, I just might . . .' She scraped a finger-nail along Jay's forearm.

He glanced at her briefcase. 'Do you have it with you now?'

'What's it worth?'

'Anything.'

Hilary thought for a moment. She thought about Riddle, with his olde-worlde snobbery and his insufferable arrogance. Yes, she would like Riddle to get in trouble with the law and have his name splashed across the newspapers. She actually *wanted* Jay to have the photograph. But she didn't want to make it easy for him. She wanted to have a little fun at his expense.

'All right. But not now – tonight. And you're going to have to be very, very nice to me . . .'

Later that afternoon, Jay slipped out of Rapier Promotions and ran down to the Prince's Theatre in Cambridge Circus.

Because rain was forecast, Hilary had expressed a desire to go out to a show that evening, but it wasn't to be *any* show, it was to be *Les Misérables*. So now he was one of many fighting to get tickets for it, including several hundred American tourists.

First he had tried phoning, but the lines were constantly engaged. He sent his secretary there in a taxi, but she came back empty-handed, so he had no choice but to go in person.

When he reached the theatre he found a crowd of disgruntled Americans on the steps, complaining that they had been turned away from the box office.

' . . . They say they got a full house and we flew all the way from New Jersey (Indianapolis/South Carolina/Arkansas) to see this show! . . .'

Jay charged up the steps and managed to slip into the foyer just as they were closing the doors. He hammered on the locked window of the box office until it was opened up again by a very sullen-looking girl painting her nails with 'Amber Dawn'.

'What?' she challenged.

'I need two tickets.'

'Sorry, no tickets left. We're closed.'

She started to lower the grille, but Jay stuck his hand in and forced it up again.

'Look . . . if you did have a couple of tickets, I'd be very grateful . . .' Jay raised and lowered his eyebrows dramatically, trying some non-verbal communication on her.

'What?' She stared at him, brush poised, until the penny dropped. 'How grateful?'

Her petulant tone reminded him of Hilary, and he decided that women really were all sisters under the skin, conspiring to make his life difficult.

'Fifty?'

'A hundred.'

He handed over the money and the girl found him the tickets, but he was forced to hand them back to her straight away. They were at the back of the upper dress circle, next to 'EXIT' and 'TOILETS'. Hilary would never tolerate that, and the whole operation might be blown. The girl then insisted that there was no refund possible on 'special tickets', so he left the theatre a hundred pounds poorer and considerably more desperate.

There was a tout outside with a pair of front row stalls for the evening performance.

'How much?' asked Jay, steeling himself.

'For you guv . . .' The tout ran a practised eye over Jay's gold Rolex and his brand-new Gucci loafers. 'Five hundred . . . each.'

'Four hundred.'

'Four fifty, and I'm robbing meself . . .'

When Jay got back to Rapier Promotions, he couldn't resist telephoning Hilary at the bank.

'Just calling to say I got the tickets . . .' (He made sure his tone was casual)' . . . cost me a thousand big ones, but I got them.'

'I can't go to the theatre tonight; I've got nothing to wear . . .'

Several phone calls later, and an ex-showroom ball gown from the Emmanuel's salon was rushed round to Boeler Sute in a taxi. Naturally Hilary looked ravishingly pretty in it, and she made sure that Jay said so when he met her for pre-theatre drinks at Trader Vic's. He, not to be outdone, was wearing a white tuxedo and black patent dress shoes.

'You know . . .' mused Hilary as they walked outside to get into his car. 'The two of us are looking so glamorous that it's rather a pity to be going to the boring old theatre . . .'

Jay thought of the three figure tickets and ground his teeth. 'Listen, babe, you wanted to go to the theatre . . .'

'That was when I thought it was going to rain. It's fine now.'

At that moment, the gods decided to take pity on Jay Cathcart. The sky darkened and heavy drops of rain began to fall.

Jay ushered Hilary towards his car, but she resisted him. She stood with her palm out, letting the rain splash onto it. Her nose wrinkled in distaste. 'Our climate is so horrid, don't you think? . . . what I'd *really* like to do is to escape it and go somewhere warm . . .'

She glanced up at Jay and a look passed between them, a look that said '*I've got what you want, so let's see how far you're prepared to go to get it* . . .'

'Wait there one second . . .' Still clutching the theatre tickets, Jay ran to his Twin-Cam Intercooler convertible and picked up the car phone. He dialled Ivo's home number.

'Have the small jet standing by!' he said and grinned. He was beginning to enjoy himself. It was the closest he would ever get to being James Bond. ' . . . If you want to own the Star Group, don't ask any questions, just do it!'

He bundled a smirking Hilary into the passenger seat, along with her briefcase and its precious cargo, and drove at ninety five miles an hour to the small airfield north east of London where Ivo kept his private light plane. Now Jay was really coming into his own. He took Hilary by the hand

and pulled her across the runway to where the jet was standing with its engines roaring, refusing to slacken his pace when she complained that he was going too fast.

'What's the matter, can't you keep up with life in the fast lane? . . .'

For just over an hour he bombarded her with Beluga caviar and vintage champagne and was just starting on the strawberries when the plane bumped on the runway and the jets died.

'Right, now we're in Monaco. Is that warm enough for you?'

A dazed and slightly green Hilary was then dragged off for a late supper on a roof-top restaurant, a clip round the coast road in a rented Maserati, two hours of black-jack at the Casino Royale and dancing at Monte Carlo's most exclusive nightclub. By the end of it she was suffering from exhaustion and hyper-glamour. Jay was winning.

For the moment.

As he turned the car towards the airport, Hilary gave him a sly, sidelong look and said: 'We don't have to rush back now, do we? I'm having such a super time I want to spend a few days here.'

Jay hesitated.

'Did you hear what I said? I said I want—'

Jay loosened his black tie, turned the car round and headed back to Monte Carlo and the Hôtel de Paris. This ruined everything, but he wasn't going to let Hilary know that. He'd told the pilot to have the plane standing by for the return flight, but the wasted expense was the least of his problems. Heidi needed that photo and she needed it now, not in two or three days time.

He wished he really *was* James Bond, and had a gun secreted under his armpit that he could point it at the silly little bitch. He racked his brains. Supposing 007 didn't have his gun, what would he do then? Of course, it was obvious. He'd go to the girl's bedroom.

Jay was about to make a startling discovery.

He checked himself and Hilary into separate rooms at the Hôtel de Pàris, closing his eyes as he signed his credit card slip. Then he sat on the edge of his bed and waited until he could be sure Hilary was asleep. Dawn was breaking as he crept down the corridor. The chambermaids were starting work.

'Hi!' he said, giving one of them his most winning grin and a hundred franc note. 'I'm afraid I've accidentally locked myself out of my room. Could you possibly lend me your pass key? . . .'

Jay let himself into Hilary's room, then paused to remove his shoes so that he would make less noise. As he did so, he heard a most curious sound coming from the direction of the bed. He listened, and there it was again, in all its unmistakable awfulness.

Hilary Ardent snored.

Not, as he might have imagined, gentle ladylike snores, or even heavy breathing, but loud, rasping snorts like an overweight sow in labour. It hardly seemed possible that such a din could come from so small and slender a body.

So there is some justice in this life, thought Jay, as he groped around in the dark for Hilary's briefcase. It was locked.

He was considering taking the whole thing with him and breaking it open, when he remembered seeing a gold chain round Hilary's neck, with a small key hanging from it. What if . . .

She was lying on her side, and the gold chain was just visible above the edge of the white satin sheet. Could he lift her hair and undo the clasp without waking her? Jay considered the deafening snores and decided he could.

He removed the key from the chain and tiptoed to where

he'd left the briefcase. Inside there was a large manila envelope resting on top of her other papers. Jay checked that it held what he was after and shoved it inside his cummerbund, he was just attempting to return the key when Hilary gave a snort and sat up.

'Jay!' she said, and was clearly not sure whether to be angry or flattered at so bald an attempt at seduction.

Jay quickly gathered his composure and ran his lips over her naked shoulder as though he found it irresistible. 'You've got such beautiful skin, babe . . .'

Hilary pushed him away, but she was smiling. 'What's the hurry, Jay? After all, we've got several days alone here, haven't we?'

'Right, right,' said Jay, trying to prevent his waistband from crackling too loudly. 'Sure. I'll, er . . . leave you to it.'

And leave her was precisely what he did. Feeling more like a double agent than ever, he phoned the airstrip from reception then ran out and hailed a cab to take him there, Hilary could keep the Maserati.

The engines were running when he arrived, and he sprinted to the cockpit and jumped in beside the pilot.

'Success?' he asked Jay as the plane hit the end of the runway.

'Mission accomplished.' Jay replied, hugging the envelope and looking down from the cockpit. 'It may not know it, but that little principality has just witnessed Jay Cathcart's finest hour.'

Eight

Jay, Heidi and Leofred were holding their third and final meeting.

This time it was not at Heidi's bedsit, or at Jay's office but in the middle of Waterloo Bridge.

It was Jay's idea.

'But why?' Heidi had asked him on the phone. 'It might be raining.'

'Aha!..' said Jay in a faraway tone.

Reflecting that Jay's lightning trip to Monte Carlo had turned him very peculiar, Heidi went to Waterloo Bridge and stood there waiting, with Leofred. It was drizzling.

'Look,' said Leofred suddenly, 'Isn't that him?'

A tall figure was sauntering towards them, affecting a casual air. He wore a trenchcoat with the collar turned up, and dark glasses splattered with rain. As he came within earshot, he hissed: *'I've got the pictures.'*

'Don't be such a jerk, Jay, just let us have a look!'

Jay took out a large envelope and the three of them stood at the centre of the bridge, trying to look at the photographs. The rain was making them soggy and the wind tore at their edges, making it impossible to flatten them.

'Christ, let's just forget the Phillip Marlowe bit and go inside!' said Heidi.

They went into a pub at the top of the Strand and huddled round a circular table with three beers and a packet of dry roasted peanuts.

'Okay kids,' said Jay, reaching inside his raincoat like a dirty old man, 'Let's have a look at what Uncle Jay's brought you!'

He glanced over his shoulder and then put Hilary's original print on the table in front of them. Heidi picked it up and examined it closely.

'It's quite good of Riddle.' she said eventually, 'And the cash. But the other bloke's got his back to the camera and he's in the shadow. It doesn't tell us much.'

'I thought of that,' said Jay, very proud of himself. 'And I had the guys in Video Editing tinker around with it a bit.'

The second print was of the mystery man alone, and it had been given more light and definition. Heidi looked carefully at the stance of the slight figure . . .

. . . And was suddenly reminded of the house in Hampstead and the shadowy figure in the window.

'It's him!' she said, becoming excited, 'It's Mr X, I'm sure of it!'

'And now . . .' said Jay with a flourish, 'The master stroke!'

He handed Heidi a third print, which was a blow-up of a tiny section of the original picture. 'A guy in the lab spotted a luggage label on his suitcase and asked if I wanted to know what it said . . .'

Heidi examined it. It was a label issued by the US airline, TWA. It was twisted so the name wasn't visible, but under 'address' was printed ' . . . *HOTEL, NEW YORK CITY.*'

'What is it?' asked Leofred nervously, recognising the transfixed expression on his sister's face.

She stared at the picture for a while, then looked up,

beaming. 'It's a risk, but it has to be our best chance at this stage.'

'Count me in,' said Jay, 'After last night I'm into risks in a big way.'

Heidi was thinking out loud. 'We already know that Hyman Weevil is in New York, in need of all the help he can get if he's to make a successful bid for Star. And Mr X – if it's him –was on his way there . . . Jay, what are the chances of your credit card tolerating three airline tickets to New York? . . .'

'*The only emotion New York cannot arouse is indifference,*' said Leofred, reading aloud from the guide book, '*No other place created by man provokes such adoration and abhorrence . . .*'

'Cut the crap,' said Heidi, shooing off a group of Puerto-Rican pre-teens who had just pick-pocketed Jay's wallet then tried to sell it back to him, 'Turn to the list of hotels. That's what we're supposed to be looking at.'

The intrepid three stood on the corner of West Forty Second and Tenth, between *The Poopie Cat Corp* and a fast food joint called 'Thinny-Thin No: Cholesterol to Go'. What seemed to be half the population of that city jogged, cycled, skated or flipped frisbees past them.

'Let's see,' said Heidi, running a jet-lagged eye down the travel guide. 'We've checked out the Barbizon-Plaza, the Howard Johnson, the Parker Meridien . . .'

'Why don't we cruise off and do us some grazing?' said Jay, who had no trouble at all slipping into New York-ese, 'Then after lunch we can walk to all the other fifty-seven hotels.'

'Let's just try a few more, *please*' begged Heidi. 'We've got the whole East Side to do yet.'

In the end they compromised. They would head east looking for somewhere to eat, and on the way if they passed a hotel one of them would go in and ask if an Englishman fitting Mr X's description had checked in recently.

The search was predictably fruitless, and they arrived at Hoexter's Cafe an hour later, exhausted and bad-tempered. Heidi's spirits were only slightly raised by the handsome waiter in a white apron and Reeboks who brought her iced water.

'Hi, my name is Dean, and I'm going to be your waiter today. How may I help you?'

Heidi blushed and stumbled over her ordering until she noticed that Dean was fluttering his eyelashes at Jay, and not at her. She ordered sweetbreads with strawberries and the others chose deep-dish designer pizzas topped with raw sturgeon and sliced figs.

'Okay,' said Heidi with a sigh, once she had polished off her Californian cuisine, 'Let's be honest, we're never going to find him this way.'

'We might try phoning round the hotels instead.' suggested Leofred.

Jay shook his head. 'No way. Not in this city. If we don't know who it is we're asking for, they're just going to think it's a crank call and hang up.'

They sat in doom-laden silence for a while, drinking cups of espresso. They were the last diners to order lunch, and the restaurant was about to close. Dean leaned against the bar, yawning, waiting for them to finish. One of the other waiters sat on a high stool, picking his ears and thumbing through the *New York Times*.

'Hang on a minute!' said Heidi suddenly, pointing at the newspaper. 'Is that what I think it is?'

On the back page of the *Times*, there was a photograph of a man in a ten-gallon hat.

'Could I take a quick look at your paper?' Heidi asked the waiter.

'Sure, go ahead.'

Heidi examined the picture and read the short article that went with it. 'It's about Hyman Weevil,' she told the others. 'It says that when he's in town, he stays at the Pierre.'

'So?' asked Jay.

Heidi was smiling. 'Well now we know where Weevil is, at least we have a chance to put my theory to the test. If I'm right, then wherever Weevil is, Mr X isn't far away. If I'm wrong, then we're wasting our time here anyway.'

'So we're going to treat Weevil like bait, you mean?' asked Leofred, 'To lure our prey?'

'Precisely. All we have to do is get chummy with Weevil.'

'And how do we do that.'

'I don't know – yet.'

Heidi lay on her bed at the Salisbury Hotel surrounded by parcels from Saks Fifth Avenue and Henri Bendel. In her left hand she had a bag of Aunt Sadie's Treble Fudge Pecan cookies and in her right, a bottle of Michelob Lite. She was watching *All My Children* and trying to figure out what Brad's nervous breakdown had to do with Norma's long lost cousin coming back from the dead.

When the plot became too intricate she switched channels to the in-house movie, and was about to settle back with '*The Thing that came out of the Swamp III*' when there was a gentle tap at her door.

Heidi opened the door and found a young woman standing opposite her with a fixed and beaming smile on her face. She carried a briefcase, and was immaculately dressed in suit, pussy-cat blouse and high heels.

'Hi, I'm Shawna . . .' The smile evaporated. 'Oh – you're not Mr Pantikoff.'

'No, I'm not.'

Shawna's eyes narrowed, and she stared at Heidi's skimpy T-shirt and bare legs. 'Well, I sure as hell hope you're not *with* Mr Pantikoff, because if you are, lady, you're on my patch!'

Heidi frowned. 'I'm not with anyone, I'm here on my own. Look, I think—'

'Gee, I'm sorry! There must have been a mix-up. Could I come in and use your phone please?'

'Be my guest . . .'

Heidi followed Shawna into the room and watched as she unclipped a baroque pearl earring and picked up the receiver.

'Hi, it's Shawna . . . yes . . . no . . . uh un . . . sure, I get it; Room 1455 instead of Room 1459 . . . okay, you'd better call me back.'

'That was the agency I work for,' she explained cheerfully, 'They're just going to sort out the mistake and call me back on this.' She indicated a radio bleeper that was attached to her waistband.

'Agency? Are you some sort of secretary?'

Shawna laughed. 'No dummy, the Elite Agency!' Seeing Heidi's puzzled expression, she went on, 'But you're new to Manhattan, aren't you, so I guess you wouldn't have heard about it. C'mere, I want to show you something . . .'

She laid her briefcase on the bed and opened the lid to display its contents. There was a cosmetics bag with miniatures of everything needed for a full make-up, a Ziploc bag containing spare pantyhose, a shower cap, a Port-a-print for processing credit cards and three packets of contraceptives.

'The Elite is Manhattan's most exclusive escort agency,' said Shawna in a rehearsed sing-song voice. 'I'm a call girl.'

'Oh . . . I see.'

Heidi stared at the briefcase with its essential requirements for the working girl, and suddenly had an idea. 'If you've got a minute, I'd love to hear what it's like. Working for the agency, I mean.'

'Sure,' said Shawna, whose real name was Betty. She sat down and eased off her shoes. 'These darn things kill me. Alison insists we wear them.'

'Alison?'

'The mada— . . . I mean, the manageress.'

'Cookie?' Heidi proffered the bag.

'Thanks.' Shawna/Betty took a couple, and the bottle of beer that Heidi handed to her.

'So you were visiting a . . .'

'Client,' prompted Shawna. 'Alison doesn't like us to say "john" or "trick". Only at the office they told me the wrong room number. On the nights of the week I'm on duty they call me at home and give me the guy's name and address. Then I take a cab downtown to his hotel or apartment and introduce myself. We get talking, maybe have a little wine, and after half an hour or so, I'll ask him if he maybe wants to get a little more comfortable. Then anything that's going to happen, happens—'

'You mean sex.' interrupted Heidi.

'Alison doesn't like us to refer to it in those terms. We're supposed to act like ladies . . . Anyhow, then I go into the bathroom and wash up, freshen my make-up, and then the guy pays. Except Alison doesn't allow us to ask directly for money, of course—'

'Of course.' Heidi munched thoughtfully on a double fudge cookie, 'How much is it?' she asked, with her mouth full.

'We accept personal cheques, Diner's Card and Visa.' said Shawna in her practised, sing-song voice, adding in a normal tone. 'And it's two-hundred-and-fifty bucks a throw. More than an hour and it's charged as extra time.'

'Quite a good way to make a living,' observed Heidi.

'Yup,' said Shawna, reverting temporarily to Betty and taking a deep draught of beer. 'And easy too, except for the grooming. That's a bit of a pain in the ass.'

The concept of grooming was alien to Heidi, who thought it was something girls with big behinds and jodphurs did at weekends.

'You know, we have to wear a silk garter belt and nylons, and our nail varnish and lipstick have to match, and we can't wear certain colours because Alison says they're too tacky.'

'I see. And is this your . . . er, career?'

'Hell no! This is my summer job, for the long vacation. I'm a law major at Cornell.' Shawna's bleeper went off and she answered it. 'That was the office, ringing to confirm that Mr Pantikoff's in his room. I'd better run . . .'

Shawna stood up, straightened her blouse and crammed her feet into the high heels. She took a little aerosol from her briefcase and squirted peppermint in her mouth to disguise the beer. 'It was nice meeting you. So long . . .'

Heidi waited for the sound of the elevator doors, then picked up the phone and dialled down to the room that the boys were sharing.

'Leof? It's me. I think I've cracked it . . .'

A yellow cab skirted Central Park and drew up on Sixty First and Fifth Avenue outside the Pierre Hotel, temporary home to monarchs and presidents.

Inside the lobby, two bellboys watched a smart young woman climb out and walk under the gold and beige awning and into the hotel. She had long chestnut hair, an Oscar de la Renta outfit and matching accessories. And a briefcase.

'I'll bet you that's one of them high class hookers,' one bellboy whispered to the other. 'Should we call security?'

'Nah.' said his friend. 'So what if she is? We're supposed to be keeping the guests happy, aren't we?'

Heidi – for it was she beneath the wig – climbed into the elevator and rode up to the top floor. She was so engrossed in balancing on her new shoes that she walked straight past the potted palm where Leofred and Jay were hiding.

Jay let out a long wolf whistle. 'Hey! Look at *you!*'

'The result of two hours in the beauty parlor,' said Heidi drily, 'And I feel like a trussed turkey.'

'You look the part though,' said Leofred. 'Ah, I mean . . . you know what I mean . . .'

'Okay, I'm going down now,' said Heidi. 'You two stay up here out of sight until you're needed, unless I'm there more than an hour, in which case I'll need rescuing. Right – here goes . . .'

She marched down a floor and tapped on one of the doors. It was opened by a small, leathery man with matching hair and teeth.

'Hi! I'm Janna!' Heidi attempted a sing-song, down-home accent.

'Say what?'

'I'm the girl you ordered from Elite,' said Heidi, forcing up the corners of her mouth and praying her wig was still straight. She just hoped that they would take enough time sorting out that she had the wrong room to allow her to do a bit of detective work.

'But I don't use Elite,' said a puzzled Hyman Weevil. 'Every time I'm in town I always call me up the Caresse agency. Monica's girls are always just fine!'

Heidi was thinking on her feet. 'Ah . . . quite right. You see, Elite and Caresse are under the same ownership now;

they've merged.' Trying to step up the plausability she added, 'Alison's bought Monica out.'

'But I spoke to Monica just five minutes ago. Said she would be sending someone round in an hour, when I was through with my meeting.'

'Of course. What I meant was, Monica's bought Alison out. Silly old me!'

Heidi affected a poor-dumb-bunny-with-no-head-for-business look.

'That a fact? Well, I guess you'd better come in then . . .'

Heidi followed him into the room and took stock of the hand-painted marble bathroom and the electronically operated window drapes.

' . . . but I don't mind telling you, I'm not happy about this, no sir. I was told I was getting me silky blonde hair and a big pair of titties. You're kind of scrawny. And I don't care for broo-nettes, neither.'

There was no time for Heidi to regret turning down the honey blonde wig the salesgirl had offered. She was panicking about the fact that Hyman Weevil had obviously planned to *use* a call girl. She hadn't quizzed Shawna about the nitty-gritty, but more worrying than that was the fact that her wig might slip off *in flagrante*.

'Tell you what,' she said, 'Why don't I call Alis – I mean, Monica at the agency and get them to send a blonde girl over'. Then you and I could just sit here and . . . well, we wouldn't have to do anything; we could just talk—'

'*Just talk!* Honey, you don't think I was planning on doing anything else, do you? I 'ain't going pleasuring no other woman while my sweet Cora-Lee's still alive. We been wed almost forty years and I've never been unfaithful to her yet!'

'But you said you always—'

'I get Monica to send her girls over jes to keep me company when I'm in town. A feller gets lonely. And I ask them to strip down to their underpanties on account of it looks kind of decorative. I like to have them draped round the room in their silkie bits, makes me feel proud as a sultan. In fact why don't I call up and get a few more of you beauties over and we can have ourselves a regular old party!'

'No!' Heidi was alarmed. 'Not that that wouldn't be very nice, of course, but didn't you say you were about to have a meeting?'

Hyman chuckled. 'I don't know how I can have forgot that, since it's the reason I came to New York! Must be your purty little face.'

Heidi gave him a simpering southern-belle smile. 'I suppose it must be your accountant, something like that?'

'Shoot no! It's more important than that! This guy's flown all the way from England, and him and me's got big business to discuss!'

Heidi's heart began to race. He was coming, today! 'I'll undress now, shall I?' she offered. 'And you and I can have a little chat before he arrives . . .'

She stripped off to her peach satin underwear, adjusted her wig and lay on the bed in as decorous a manner as she could.

'You know, you remind me of a little girl I used to know back home in Kentucky,' said Hyman, settling back in his chair with his hat on his lap. 'She and I used to go and play up there in the mountains. We built ourselves a tree house in the branches of a hiccory, and we used to climb on up there . . . we'd look down and see that smoky old valley down below, with the mills and factories . . . and beyond that the shanty town where the niggers lived . . . and beyond that the railroads and flatcars . . .'

Weevil stood up and began to pace the room. Heidi yawned.

' . . . sometimes, on a windy day you could smell the

beef jerky and the corn bread our mommas was cooking down the valley . . . but most of the time there was too much smog. And I looked at them paper factories and I said to Mary-Lou, (that was her name, see) 'One day I'm going to have me my own paper factory and I'm going to do something real special with it. And I did. I hit on using it for incontinence pads.'

'And Mary-Lou?'

'Hell, Mary-Lou married a Baptist preacher and had herself six kids. And I met Cora-Lee. But I always remembered Mary Lou . . . just like you she was, with them long brown curls.'

Hymen reached out and fondled the wig, then resumed pacing. 'I'm kinda nervous I guess. There's a lot riding on this meeting . . .' He checked his watch.

The phone rang.

'Honey, I guess you'd better start smartening up. That was reception to say he's arrived and he'll be up in five minutes. But I thank you for your time.' Hyman doffed his enormous hat and did a little bow.

Heidi started flinging on her clothes with an indecent haste that would have enraged Alison or Monica. As soon as Hyman disappeared into the bathroom she grabbed her briefcase and ran out of the room, almost knocking over a tall buxom blonde.

'Hi! I'm Blaine from Caresse—'

'You're too late!' shouted Heidi as she tore down the corridor, 'I mean, too early!'

She ran up the stairs to the top floor and shook the potted palm violently to flush out Jay and Leofred!'

'It's Mr X!' she gasped, once she could speak. 'Quick! He's coming up in the lift!'

The three of them raced down a floor, Heidi with her blouse unfastened and her wig slipping over one ear, reaching the elevator as it arrived on that floor.

They positioned themselves by the doors, waiting as they slid smoothly open . . .

. . . and out stepped a man in a sharkskin suit and dark glasses.

'My God!' said Leofred faintly. 'It's you!'

Nine

Mr X stood motionless before them as the elevator doors clanged shut. For a few seconds he didn't move a muscle in his massive frame. Then he lifted his shades to reveal sapphire blue eyes – not unlike Paul Newman's – in a craggy weatherbeaten face.

With a curl of his lip he reached inside his jacket and pulled out a .45 revolver . . .

With some reluctance, Heidi drifted back from her fantasy to her room in the Salisbury Hotel. She lifted her dry martini to her lips and gulped it down in a resigned fashion. She, Jay and Leofred were having cocktails and a post-mortem with the real Mr X, who turned out to be a callow, spotty Old Godborian by the name of Dave Jelling.

Heidi tried to suppress her disappointment and pay attention to Dave's account of how he had become an infamous international arbitrageur.

'. . . anyway, then the recruitment bandwagon came to town and I steered well clear, but one night there was a rumour going round in the college buttery that someone was looking for a student with knowledge of the stock market to undertake a special short term commission. Lots of dosh. So I put my name forward and this guy came to see me one night.'

'Oliver Riddle.' Heidi interjected with satisfaction. 'It has to be.'

'Yeah, that's right.' Dave looked suitably impressed. 'The heat was on him and he wanted out of the kitchen. So he set me up to buy Star stock, and to find buyers for Drummond stock . . .' Dave shrugged. 'I mean, it was so easy. The system was ripe to be exploited. And soon other guys started ringing me, and the money was rolling in, and I thought hey shit, this is all running a bit fast—'

'And Hyman Weevil?' demanded Heidi. 'Is he one of your clients?'

'That's right.' Dave glanced at his watch. 'At this very moment I'm supposed to be helping the geezer buy into Star's companies, in time for him to offer for the whole group.'

Leofred frowned. 'Isn't it a bit late in the day? Why should he do that now?'

'It was Riddle's idea.'

'*Riddle?* But—'

'Yeah, Oliver Riddle. He was the one who came up with Weevil's name at the last minute. As soon as Clive Fender cracked up and Drummond was looking dodgy, he dumped them. But Riddle's a greedy guy and he didn't want all his hard work to go to waste. He found someone rich enough to start buying out Drummond's share in Star, undoing all the work he'd done for Fender, but making sure he wasn't going to lose out. If Weevil succeeds, he's going to make Riddle chairman and give him a huge chunk of voting stock.'

Heidi shook her head slowly, and sighed. 'And I thought old Hyman seemed rather a sweetie.'

'He is,' said Dave. 'Riddle's just using him. He's dead naive – I don't think he really knows what he was about to get into. I don't think he really *wants* the Star Group. He's just got more money than he knows what to do with.'

'I think he ought to stick to throwing parties for call girls.' said Heidi.

She mixed them all another round of martinis, after which Dave cleared his throat and enquired a little nervously if she was going to 'shop' him.

Heidi had momentary thoughts about crime, punishment and justice, but she was a journalist after all, so they were only momentary. 'No,' she said, 'Not if you'll help me with my story. I'm going to need precise details – times, dates, figures . . . names.'

Dave looked at Leofred, who nodded. 'Sure – why not? I've made a six figure sum in six weeks. I've exploited the establishment. And I don't give a monkey's who owns the Star Group. I just want to have a good time.'

'All *right!*' whooped Jay, with whom he had struck a chord at last.' That's cool!'

'I think the time has come for us to drink a toast,' said Heidi, raising her martini glass.

' . . . to the unmasking of Mr X!'

Leofred returned from his forty-eight hours in New York with a double dose of jet lag. He hadn't been able to get over flying west over the Atlantic before he flew east again. His brain felt like a particularly tough piece of airline meat.

He let himself into his bedsit and tripped over a pile of hostile letters from his bank manager and opportunities to win twenty-five thousand pounds in a Reader's Digest draw. They had left for New York in such a hurry that the room was in a state of suspended animation. The sheets on the bed still had the imprint of his body, and the carton of milk was on the fridge where he had left it, only now it was cottage cheese.

He stumbled around the room for a while, like a dog

turning in its basket, then flopped onto the bed and closed his eyes.

The phone rang.

'*Hiya darlin'!*'

Leofred grunted.

'*It's Sandra! Have you just got back?*'

Leofred grunted again.

'*In that case you've got back just in time for the party! I've got the piccies back from Boots, and me and the Girls are having a Fuengirola reunion. So come on down!*'

'Sandra, you don't understand, I've been on a plane half the day and—'

'*You great wimp! It's only seven o'clock, isn't it? And it won't be the same without you. You and me are partners in crime, remember! And the girls will be ever so disappointed . . .*'

'All right, all right,' said Leofred, his brow well and truly beaten and his brain too addled to make a rational defence. 'I'll be there in an hour.'

He took the train to Norbury Heath and staggered to the front door of Sandra's neo-Georgian abode. There were no lights on in the house, and no-one answered the neo-Georgian door chimes. He wondered whether in his dazed state he had walked up the wrong path. After all, the houses were all identical.

Then he noticed that the door wasn't closed properly. He pushed it open.

'*Surprise, surprise!*'

The lights blazed, the stereo struck up 'E viva espana' and the Girls leapt from under the stairs wearing their Spanish sombreros. Sandra was squeezed into a flounced flamenco frock and had a rose between her teeth.

As for Doreen, Leofred didn't think he would have recognised her even if he'd been awake. She'd been on a spending spree with the money from Fender. Her hair was teased into a nest of curls and tinted a pinky colour, and she was wearing a tight purple suit and a blouse with a frothing lace jabot. A battery of cheap costume jewellery flashed under Sandra's neo-Georgian chandeliers.

Once the Girls had recovered from their delight at surprising Leofred, who in his current state was beyond being surprised, they proceeded to drown themselves in a sea of sangria.

'Good, this stuff, isn't it?' said Sandra as she brought in a third bowl full. 'I found it in Safeway's.'

The Spanish finger buffet, wheeled in on a trolley, did Sandra credit. She had prepared dainty little meatballs, marinated mushrooms and tortilla that was better than anything they had eaten in Fuengirola.

Once they had wiped their fingers on co-ordinating paper napkins, the photos were passed around, amid repeated cries of 'Ooh! D'you remember when/who/how? . . .' After several pints of sangria, all animosity and rivalry was forgotten and Debbie and Sandra giggled together over pictures of Miguel.

It was only when the others had gone that Sandra became morose.

'Look at him!' she said holding up a picture of the treacherous Spaniard. She addressed Leofred, who was slumped on the dralon sofa, too exhausted to take himself home. 'Slimy little dago! Two-timing little git!'

Under the influence of alcohol her moods were changing rapidly. She became philosophical. 'Oh well I suppose it wasn't his fault. All's fair in love and war, eh, sunshine? You win some, you lose some. I've told a few to hit the road myself. That's the name of the game when you're young and fancy free, eh? . . . eh?'

She poked Leofred in the ribs.

'Huh? . . . oh – yes.'

Sandra tugged down the front of her dress and primped her hair. 'I am attractive though, aren't I?' she inquired.

Philosophy suddenly gave way to insecurity. '*You* think I am, don't you darlin'?'

Her cleavage loomed close to Leofred's face. 'Don't you?'

'Ah . . . yes.'

'Good . . .' Sandra snuggled close. 'I always thought you rather fancied me . . .'

Her hand was on his crotch. Leofred lay motionless, too tired to believe what was happening.

' . . . These button fly jeans really are a nuisance . . . they don't half keep a girl guessing . . .'

But Sandra was guessing in vain. Leofred's member lay limply in her hand. She hitched up her flamenco dress and tried a bit of pressure from her thighs, but it resolutely refused to budge.

'Sorry . . .' muttered Leofred. 'Jet lag . . .'

To his horror Sandra began to cry noisily.

' . . . s'not all it's cracked up to be, this single lark . . .' Her nose ran and saliva bubbled in her mouth as she tried to talk. ' . . . you run around pretending to be having a great time, but sometimes I just get so . . . lonely.'

'I'm sorry,' Leofred kept repeating, 'I'm sorry.'

''Snot your fault.' Sandra sobbed. 'I mean, you didn't really want to, did you? I forced you, stupid old cow that I am . . . trying to act nineteen when I'm going to be forty next birthday . . .'

'Look Sandra, perhaps I'd better go—'

'No! No, please don't!' She scrubbed hastily at the rings of mascara underneath her eyes, 'Please stay the night. I get so bloody fed up with sleeping alone. I just want someone to bring a cup of tea to in the morning, that's all.'

She led Leofred upstairs, and helped him to undress. 'Clumsy bugger,' she said fondly. 'Come on. You hop in here . . .'

Sandra folded back the satinette bedspread and spent

some time ensuring he was 'comfy'. Then she slipped in beside him.

Leofred gave a grateful sigh, curled up in Sandra's arms and slept like a baby.

While Leofred slept, Heidi was awake and sitting at her desk.

Her article was due in at the *Meteor* the next day, and besides, she was too excited to sleep.

Dave Jelling had given her all she could possibly need for an eye-opening and completely damning article; details of transactions, the sums involved, the bank accounts where illegal pay-offs were deposited, phoney off-shore companies. She was also able to give any details she liked about Mr X – except his name. She agreed to let him keep his anonymity after some pleading from Leofred. It would make a far meatier article if she could name him, but in return for not doing so Dave had promised to give at least half his earnings to a charity of his choice. All concerned thought this was a fair compromise.

Heidi cracked open a can of beer, ran her fingers through her spiky hair a few times, then poised her hands over her old manual typewriter.

'*The place is one of New York's most exclusive hotels; the time mid-afternoon. On a quiet upper floor, a door opens and a girl steps out into the corridor. She is dressed like a top call-girl, in an expensive suit and high heels. Her long chestnut curls bounce as she walks . . .* '

Heidi hovered for a moment, and then thought, why not? She could allow herself a little poetic licence.

' *. . . She is stunningly beautiful.*

On the way to the lift, the girl passes a young Englishman.

He has business with the client she has just left, who also happens to be one of America's leading industrialists . . . '

Heidi paused for a moment, wondering how she could conclude the conjectured scene. Should she get in with a few names now, or should she only reveal them at the end? . . .

She took another swig of beer and tapped a biro on the edge of the desk. Then something caught her eye; a piece of *Meteor* headed stationery. She picked it up and looked at it. It was an official memo she had been typing when she dropped everything to rush off to New York.

'TO THE HEAD OF PICTURES:
I would like to draw your attention to the matter of the age limit in the Chick of The Year contest. The stated category is for girls aged 16–19. However, it has recently been brought to my notice that one of the short listed entrants has already celebrated her twentieth birthday. She is Sammi-Dawn Thwort, of Plumstead, East London—'

Heidi laughed aloud at this uncharacteristic piece of pomposity. Then she screwed the half-finished memo into a ball and, still laughing, tossed it into the waste-paper bin.

The next day, at Juniper House, the employees of Drummond Industries were preparing for a board meeting.

It was to be no ordinary meeting. It stirred more than the usual amount of dread in some, and a great deal of excitement in others. All morning internal phones rang frantically, people ran up and down stairs and there was loud whispering in the ladies cloakroom.

At two o'clock precisely, Leofred Plunkett left his office and walked to the Typing Pool. Sandra and Doreen were sitting at their desks, waiting.

'Ready?' asked Leofred.

The three of them set off in the direction of the board-room, walking with a firm purposeful tread.

'Good luck mate!' shouted Ray Doyle, sticking his head round the door of his office and letting the fag fall from his mouth onto the carpet. Even Erica Whittie gave them a faint smile as they marched resolutely by.

It was only when they got to the door of the boardroom that there was a moment of hesitation.

'Oooer!' complained Doreen. 'I've got butterflies!'

Sandra put her hand on Leofred's arm as he reached for the door handle, and for the first time ever, he saw her blush. 'About last night – can we just forget about it, eh?'

'Consider it forgotten.'

'Still mates?'

'Still mates.'

Leofred led the way into the oak-panelled boardroom, and the three of them took their places at the top of the table, facing the directors. The turn-out was poor. Not only was the chairman conspicuous in his absence, but also several of his fellow board members, whose share portfolios had blossomed as a result of inside information. They had sent their apologies from Guernsey, Panama and the Cayman Islands. Those who remained were Taylor, Oxenwell, Neave and Scott-Pine; four big men in chalk pinstripes with dandruff on the collar and a worried look in the eye.

'Right, gentlemen' Leofred stood up and opened a folder. It had nothing but doodles in it, but it made him look more important. 'First I'd better explain why we're here.'

The boring hours spent reading through company records had paid off at last. He had discovered a very useful piece of information.

'I'd like to remind you of item 336a in the list of company protocols. It says that in the absence of a board member from a meeting without due warning in writing, any employee of the company may volunteer in their place, provided they have the signature of two sponsors.'

Item 336a said exactly that, and from what Leofred could discover, it had never been overruled. Taylor, Oxenwell and co. were not going to admit that they had never heard of it, or that they didn't realise it was dated 1856, when Drummond had comprised only a few people.

'Here are the signatures sponsoring myself, Mrs Thwort—' he indicated Doreen, 'and Mrs Snell.' He indicated Sandra, who glared at the other board members.

'Shall we go on to the first item on the agenda; the election of a new chairman?'

Taylor, Oxenwell, Neave and Scott-Pine nodded weakly.

'You all know the form – candidates are nominated in advance and their names circulated to all board members. Then we put it to the vote. I see someone has nominated Mr Oxenwell. Would anyone care to vote for him? . . .'

Scott-Pine and Taylor raised their hands a little sheepishly.

'Two votes . . . Now, you've all been informed of my nomination. As well as being a loyal employee, this is a person of sound common sense, resourcefulness and great qualities of leadership—'

'Now hang on a minute,' said Neave angrily, 'You surely can't be serious?'

'Hear, hear!' said Oxenwell, 'The idea is quite absurd. A mere—'

'May I also remind you,' Leofred went on, as if he hadn't heard. 'That Mrs Thwort here has a very interesting story to tell about a certain company car that went missing. She's been offered a lot of money by a tabloid newspaper for that exact same story. I'm sure none of us want Drummond being dragged through this sort of scandal, let alone a closer inspection of the system of company perks . . .'

The board members paled. Neave cleared his throat. 'Of course not . . .'

'*That's the way to do it!*' hissed Sandra, '*Go for the goolies!*'

'So, can I ask those who support my nomination to please raise their hands?'

Doreen's shot up straightaway, followed reluctantly by Scott-Pine's. Oxenwell thought of his golf club membership and raised his.

'Thank you. And now a word from the new chairman of Drummond Industries . . .

. . . Mrs Sandra Snell.'

'Gentlemen, this is the delightful young lady I was telling you about – Miss Ardent.'

In the thickly-carpeted boardroom of Boeler Sute Merchant Bank, the directors were holding a special meeting.

Hilary Ardent stood before them, her feet neatly together and her hands folded, like an obedient schoolgirl.

So here I am at last, in here . . .

She looked at the circle of faces, flushed crimson with the effort of digesting a sumptuous directors' lunch. One chair, at the centre of the table, was empty.

' . . . Don't be deceived by that pretty face, or – if I might say so – that pretty figure. This is the very same young lady who has saved the integrity of our bank . . .'

Hilary smiled, despising them.

Incompetent, lecherous old farts . . .

The chairman, Vere Sute, swallowed an indigestion tablet and went on: 'It was through Miss Ardent's conscientious and vigilant efforts that this picture came to our attention—' He showed the still from the security camera. 'Her prompt action enabled us to deal with the crisis quickly, and more importantly, quietly. We were able to effect the unfortunate departure of our colleague, Riddle, with the minimum of argument, and no media coverage whatever. In recognition of her loyalty we propose to raise her salary and offer her a promotion—'

'I don't want a promotion.' Hilary raised her arm and pointed. 'I want that chair.'

The directors considered the empty chair from all angles, back and front, trying to work out why it was so special.

'I want to be made a director of this bank.'

They stared. One or two who had been fumbling with cigar cutters, woke up and paid attention.

'My dear young lady . . .' Vere Sute's face moved through shades of crimson to a delicate puce.

'Don't forget I still have a copy of that photo. And . . . there were several other very interesting pictures on the video tape.' lied Hilary.

Vere Sute had visions of himself and his executive secretary, embracing in the lift. 'Well of course, when we said promotion, what we meant was . . .'

Hilary Ardent left work that day as the first woman director of Boeler Sute Merchant Bank.

As she rode down in the lift, and sauntered through reception with her head in the air, she waited for people to rush up to her and offer their congratulations. No-one did. They were either too intimidated, or too jealous.

Hilary stopped at the security booth. Only old Lionel was there, with his cap on the back of his head, drinking a bottle of milk stout.

'Umm . . .' Hilary looked over her shoulder to make sure no-one was listening. 'Do you know where Steve is?'

'Steve? 'Snot 'ere.'

'Yes, I can see that. But where is he?'

'Haven't you heard?'

'Heard?'

'He's been promoted. For helping catch that git Riddle with his hands in the till. He's been moved over to our West End office.'

'Oh, I see.'

Avoiding Lionel's curious stare, Hilary fixed a smile on her lips and walked out of the building. She stopped at Lansbury's wine bar and bought a bottle of Vollereaux to take home. Bugger Steve anyway, she thought, common little oik . . .

When she got back to Highbury, she switched on her answering machine, but there were no messages. Flicking through her address book, she considered and rejected several Cambridge acquaintances that she hadn't bothered with for months. Instead she dialled Jay Cathcart's number.

'Hello Jay, it's Hilary . . . you haven't been in touch since Monaco . . . you thought I would be furious that you dumped me there? (*tinkling little laugh*) . . . of course I'm not! . . . I thought it was quite a good joke, actually . . . listen, I'm having a little party here, why don't you come over? . . . you can't make it? . . . oh, not to worry, there's loads of other people coming, of course . . . bye.'

Hilary stared at the phone for a moment. Other women would invite their girlfriends over at a moment like this. But Hilary didn't have girlfriends. She only had admirers . . .

She picked up the receiver again, and dialled Oliver Riddle's home number. He slammed the phone down on her.

Removing the champagne cork was difficult for such fragile, feminine fingers, but eventually it yielded. Then Hilary Ardent sat down and celebrated her victory, alone.

*

Ivo Cathcart sat at his desk in Rapier House, reading the latest issue of the *Daily Meteor*.

On the centre pages there was a touched-up, soft-focus photo of Heidi, with 'EXCLUSIVE' blazoned beneath it. Heidi was smiling. Ivo smiled back at her. Then he started to read the first paragraph, in heavy type, of what editors like to call 'colour writing'.

. . . the girl passes a young Englishman. He has business with the client she has just left, who also happens to be one of America's leading industrialists.

This scene is part of the final chapter in a remarkable story. It is a story that starts in Cambridge, England with a meeting between top banker Oliver Riddle and an unknown 21-year-old undergraduate. The chapters unfold like the plot of a super-soap, with power games, beautiful women, and above all, vast sums of cash . . .

The phone rang, but Ivo was so engrossed that he let his secretary answer.

She came into his office, smiling broadly. 'That was the call you were waiting for, Mr Cathcart . . . Mr Cathcart?'

Ivo looked up, reluctantly.

'It was the managing director of Star. Ringing to offer his congratulations. The company's yours.'

Ronnie Thwort was breaking up slabs of concrete to make crazy paving stones.

It was exhausting work. He straightened up to rub his back and found himself face to face with his neighbour at number 34, who was peering over the fence and grinning like a primate on heat.

'I reckon congratulations are in order, Ron!'

'Come again?'

'Don't tell me you haven't seen *this?*' He held up a copy of the *Daily Meteor*.

Ronnie snatched it from him, and flicked open the front page. 'Bleedin 'ell! . . . Doreen! *Doreen!*'

He ran up the unfinished path and into the lounge. Under Drummond's new management, Doreen had been given her first day off in thirty years. She was sitting under a dome-shaped salon dryer, eating Edinburgh rock. Her mother was watching repeats of *Play School*.

''Ere, look at this, gel!'

Doreen didn't hear, and went on munching her rock.

'I've seen this one before,' complained Doreen's mother.

'I SAID LOOK AT THIS!' Ronnie pulled the plug out of the dryer and wheeled the dome away from Doreen's head.

Doreen opened the *Meteor* and looked. There, making the best possible use of the new colour technology, were Sammi-Dawn's breasts.

'We proudly present our Chick of the Year for 1986, Miss Sammi-Dawn Thwort, 19. Super sizzling Sammi is just a home-loving girl whose hobbies include music, interior decorating and caring for pets. So get a look at Sammi's finer points, fellas!'

'What does that say?' said Doreen, squinting, 'Interior decoratin'? What's that then?'

She looked at the picture again, smoothing the paper proudly.

'Yes, well . . . I'm glad. Don't care for the nood stuff much, but I'm glad.'

'So am I.' said Ronnie, throwing Tiny a stick of Edinburgh rock. 'At least now she'll stop her bleedin' sulkin'!'

*

Many thousands of miles away, a jumbo jet was coming in to land on the runway at Rio de Janeiro, Brazil.

Among the crowd of passengers jostling their way through the customs gate was an elderly man in a false nose and beard and a smart, suntanned woman in a white leather trouser suit.

This rather unlikely couple, both in dark glasses, queue-jumped to the head of the taxi rank and sped away from the airport to the hills above the city. The taxi driver had seen many cases like this one, and understood that they were in a hurry. He was young and virile-looking, and Marjorie Fender exchanged glances with him in the rear-view mirror.

The cab drew up outside a long, low whitewashed building screened discreetly by jacarandas. 'ANNUN-CIATA CLINIC' read the sign outside.

'Here we are, Clive dear.' said Marjorie, patting her husband's hand. 'Nothing to worry about now. You're going to have a nice long rest . . .'

'No . . . no thank you. I'm quite sure.'

Heidi Plunkett put the phone down after telling the *Financial Times* that she didn't want to leave the *Meteor* and join their staff. Her shoulders slumped. She was exhausted.

She surveyed the scene in her bedsit. As usual, it was in chaos, with paper flowing from her desk like lava from Vesuvius. But today the untidiness oppressed her. She didn't have the energy to enjoy it; she didn't even have the energy to clear a space on the bed so that she could go to sleep.

Ross Hopper had offered to hold a party for her at the Groucho Club that evening, but Heidi had declined. What she needed, she decided, was to get away. She had no idea where, as long as it was far away from London. She found her suitcase under an alpine range of dirty washing and started to pack. As she performed this most solitary of tasks it occurred to her that she didn't really want to go away alone. There was always Jay, or Leofred . . . but in the end they were ruled out. She had been in their company too often of late.

Catching a glance of herself in the mirror, Heidi was horrified to see that she looked not dissimilar to the pile of dirty clothes she had just moved. After hunting out a fresh pair of jeans, she scrubbed her face in the basin, put on some lipstick and some blusher and combed her hair. Now she looked clean and tired.

There was an authoritative knock at the door. Heidi opened it and found Ivo standing there, trying to look humble but making a bad job of it. He looked far too much like a man who had just acquired a two billion pound company.

'You look nice – were you expecting someone?'

'No.'

Ivo walked into the room and viewed the half-packed suitcase.

'Going away?'

'Yes.'

'Good. You're just in time to make use of my new toy. I wanted to show it to you, anyway.'

With not a murmur of dissent, Heidi allowed Ivo to carry her suitcase out to the Bentley, which drove them to the Rapier offices. When they got out of the elevator. Ivo led them straight past his office and to the fire escape at the end of the corridor.

'It's on the roof.' he explained.

'It' was a brand new Westland chopper, white with 'CATHCART I' on the side in red letters. The huge blades were already whirling, making a deafening noise.

'Can I give you a lift somewhere?' Ivo shouted.

'Where?'

'Wherever it is you're going.'

Heidi thought for a moment. Europe seemed the best bet. There was always Paris, but she couldn't stand the French . . .

'How about Amsterdam?'

'Amsterdam it is. Hop in. And mind your head . . .'

The two of them settled in the front seat beside the pilot.

'I'm glad you got Star.' shouted Heidi as the engine was primed for take-off. The chopper lurched backwards and upwards into the air. She grabbed Ivo's hand and held onto it.

'Will you move back to the apartment, Heidi?'

Heidi shook her head. 'You'd only try and turn me into a hausfrau. We get on with our lives much better if we have separate places.'

'I see . . .' Ivo considered this, and couldn't disagree. ' . . . But can I park my car outside your house for the night, sometimes?'

'I expect so.' Heidi squeezed his hand, then looked away.

The helicopter flew low over the Thames, heading south. It flew over the warehouse in Vauxhall where Dave Jelling had just promised to donate two-hundred-thousand pounds to the Retired Guitarists Fund, and was now ringing around trying to find a drummer for his new band. It turned east, and flew over Kennington. Directly below, in Juniper House, Chairman Sandra had just decreed free hairdressing for all, and Erica Whittie had just slapped Ray Doyle's face because he asked her out to lunch. Continuing east, it passed 32 Ingledew Road, Plumstead, where Sammi-Dawn had emerged from her sulk and was treating her parents to a celebratory bottle of Babycham.

Finally it wheeled round in a circle and hovered over the City of London, that great temple to the twin gods of speculation and greed. They were so low that through plate glass windows, brokers could be glimpsed broking, bankers banking and typists typing.

Heidi leaned towards the window and sniffed the air. 'Can't you smell it?' she asked.

'Smell what?'

She laughed. 'All that cash, of course!'

Candy Barr
Hang-ups £2.50

Playboy Jay Cathcart has a Twin-Cam Turbo-Charged Intercooler Convertible, more blondes than he knows what to do with, and a total lack of finesse.

His brother, Ivo Cathcart, is Britain's youngest billionaire. He hasn't the looks, but his gilt-edged propositions get him everywhere with women . . .

Except with Heidi Plunkett. She plans game shows, has a married TV producer for a boyfriend, and the sort of sloppy good-looks that men like Ivo would give the world to wake up next to. Failing that, seventy-five grand to lift up her tee shirt.

Heidi has a brother, too: Leofred Plunkett. Sick of being ignored by the Cambridge social set, he heads for Hollywood – and unrivalled stardom in the world's worst soap opera.

Between them they have more HANG-UPS than Joan Collins' wardrobe. And even more romantic entanglements than Joan Collins . . .

'A funny, deft and highly enjoyable satire of the awful Eighties' JOHN MORTIMER

Candy Barr
Sexy £2.50

Some are born with it, some achieve it – and some have it thrust upon them . . .

Leofred Plunkett, ex-soap star and corporation mogul, is making a bid for the big time in the kissogram business. With typical commercial acumen, he's taken on fat, frumpy failure Joan Grimmins – beneath whose shapeless cardy beats a heart with a single burning desire. One day, she's going to be SEXY!

Meanwhile, Heidi Plunkett thinks she can hear wedding bells when footloose playboy Jay Cathcart dates the same blonde twice. So, too, does topless model and aspiring pop star Sammi-Dawn Thwort – as she stumbles out of the Ladies' at Jay's nightclub and into the arms of an Aussie Adonis.

All of which leads Heidi's billionaire boyfriend, Ivo Cathcart, to consider matrimony again himself . . . in between business deals.

Ivo thinks he's discovered the marketing prospect of the '80s: a contraceptive that's also a steamy aphrodisiac – and he's ready to sink all Rapier Industries' multinational assets into the launch. Nothing short of a repeat of the Stock Market crash of 1929 can stop it. And that could never happen . . . could it?

The third and final novel in the adventures of the Cathcarts and the Plunketts.

All Pan books are available at your local bookshop or newsagent, or can be ordered direct from the publisher. Indicate the number of copies required and fill in the form below.

Send to: **CS Department, Pan Books Ltd., P.O. Box 40,
Basingstoke, Hants. RG21 2YT.**

or phone: 0256 469551 (Ansaphone), quoting title, author
and Credit Card number.

Please enclose a remittance* to the value of the cover price plus: 60p for the first book plus 30p per copy for each additional book ordered to a maximum charge of £2.40 to cover postage and packing.

*Payment may be made in sterling by UK personal cheque, postal order, sterling draft or international money order, made payable to Pan Books Ltd.

Alternatively by Barclaycard/Access:

Card No. ☐☐☐☐☐☐☐☐☐☐☐☐☐☐☐☐☐☐

Signature:

Applicable only in the UK and Republic of Ireland.

While every effort is made to keep prices low, it is sometimes necessary to increase prices at short notice. Pan Books reserve the right to show on covers and charge new retail prices which may differ from those advertised in the text or elsewhere.

NAME AND ADDRESS IN BLOCK LETTERS PLEASE:

....

Name —————————————————————————————————

Address ————————————————————————————————

——————————————————————————————————————

——————————————————————————————————————

——————————————————————————————————————

3/87